Charli  . .

Lanre Fehintola was born in London of Nigerian descent. He is a photojournalist who specialises in documenting the way real people live. He has one son and lives in Bradford.

Charlie Says . . .

Don't Get High on Your Own Supply

Lanre Fehintola

Scribner

First published in Great Britain by Scribner, 2000
An imprint of Simon & Schuster UK Ltd
A Viacom Company

Scribner and design are trademarks of Macmillan Library Reference
USA, Inc., used under licence by Simon & Schuster,
the publisher of this work.

1 3 5 7 9 10 8 6 4 2

Simon & Schuster UK Ltd
Africa House
64-78 Kingsway
London WC2B 6AH

Simon & Schuster Australia
Sydney

A CIP catalogue record for this book is available
from the British Library

ISBN 0-684-86012-0

Names of people portrayed in this book have been changed
to protect the identities of the individuals.

Typeset by SX Composing DTP, Rayleigh, Essex
Printed and bound in Great Britain by Cox & Wyman Ltd, Reading, Berks

This book is dedicated to:
My two secret weapons, Olufemi and Jason Wesley

Acknowledgements

I would like to thank all those in the Manningham area who participated in the making of this book. You know who you are – your contributions were my constant companion.

Thanks also to: Shirley Stewart my agent; Martin Fletcher and everyone at Simon & Schuster for their faith and guidance; Sue Tyson; Dr Michael Ross at the Bradford DDC; Gregg Watson at the NMPFT for his interest and suggestions.

Special thanks to Leo Regan and Neil McCormick.

Contents

Preface

Charlie Says . . . has been a work in progress for some time. In fact, many of the incidents and accounts revealed in these pages were recorded on film, for a documentary that was screened on Channel 4 in October 1998. The documentary was narrated, filmed and directed by Leo Regan, a good friend and sometime partner in investigative journalism projects.

The documentary was controversial and dealt explicitly with the experiences, desires and downfalls of a community of heroin addicts in Bradford. But it was much more than good TV. What Leo presented was an unflinching recording of the real. And since I was consulted at every stage of its making, I trusted in his work. I could never have done so with a stranger, since the documentary was a recording of my life at a critical moment.

Real life is far more interesting than anything I could imagine. My work as a photojournalist has always been concerned with real people whose lives have been lost somewhere along the way. People whose stories are seldom told, because they constitute the underbelly of society. People who are regarded as unsavoury to respectable people and the Establishment generally. Yet this was where I found myself when I began to take heroin. And it's a very easy place to get to.

So truth can be stranger than fiction, but it must also be more responsible. And that is why this book is sometimes harder to swallow than a lot of fiction. Because this is what it's like to be a junkie. I'm not interested in sentimentalising experience, so if *Charlie Says . . .* leaves a bad taste in a few mouths, so be it.

There are several main characters in this book, whose experiences were recorded over a number of years through photos, film, tape and notes. Their depictions are as true as someone's life can be when viewed through another's eyes – especially when that person is as addicted and desperate as those he is trying to represent.

Some of the characters, such as Giant, Maureen and Ellie, appear several times in different states of mind and addiction. Their stories have a narrative thread, their lives a sense of history and development. However, their stories can also be read in isolation, since the book is intended to be episodic in the same way that a documentary might be. My own stories are those with descriptive titles such as 'The Visit' or 'Drugs Bust'. The scenes headed 'Conversation' always take place at Lance and Ellie's flat.

The documentary, be it film, literature or television, has become very popular over the last decade. It is successful because it seems authentic and validates voyeurism. But, while film makers aren't usually implicated in the footage, or writers in the text, for me this 'get out clause' was never an option. Because I was writing from within the text, I was part of the picture.

Lanre: The Twilight Zone

Driving round town working my shift. Rushing to and from punters, setting up deals, for almost seventy-two hours non-stop and without a wink of sleep. I was dog tired. My head was so fuckin' wired there was just no space left to deal with the demands for more cocaine. Seventy-two hours of serious hustling, contesting hundreds of different attitude problems. Had to stop immediately if my sanity was to survive. But then a call came over the mobile for a sixteenth, which would mean another £100 in my pocket . . . So instead of rushing off home, as I should've done, I pulled up at the kerb and discreetly built myself a spliff.

I know I shouldn't have, but crack, mixed with a sprinkling of heroin to take away the edginess, was just what I needed to give myself that extra boost of energy before setting off again. But the revival was only short lived and very soon I was feeling even more wasted than I had a few moments before. So I built myself another spliff. In fact I built two, and smoked them straight off, one after the other.

It was a dangerous game I was playing, trying to

balance the extremities of my consciousness whilst hurtling through the city centre at more than twice the legal speed limit. Using drugs to ward off sleep – though sometimes drugs are better than sleep – was like teetering on a knife edge somewhere between the light and dark. And it was just at that moment I realised I was in the grip of some unreal force.

Bang in the middle of a traffic jam on the Queens Road, the lights seemed forever stuck on red and I was nodding off at the wheel again. I could feel a mist of sleep descending like a veil over my eyes, obscuring my vision and making my senses dull and uncoordinated. That last spliff definitely hadn't worked, and shaking my head to try to see a way through my confusion didn't help either. Through the corner of my eye I could just make out someone in the next lane making frantic hand gestures at me.

Maybe I know them, I thought. *Maybe it's the punter I'm supposed to be meeting.* I turned to look at them full-on but found myself staring into an empty space, dark like I had my eyes closed. In that darkness I could half see, half imagine myself sitting there in the driver's seat disintegrating, almost disappearing into its fabric. As if my whole body was shrinking away from a business in which it was no longer able to participate . . . like I'd fallen into a black hole.

Then further, much deeper into the darkness, where the black finally succumbs to lesser tones and shadowy figures begin to emerge from a landscape of dreams, I am struck by a memory of myself, eighteen years ago, sitting in the very same traffic jam. I remember how I enjoyed the thrill of racing up and down in a sports car stolen the previous night and how I was feeling supremely confident. I recognise the excitement, the buzz, and that adrenaline-rush through my veins, like a tidal wave. Then I remember how suddenly that confidence burst when the traffic lights changed, and how I dared not release the hand-brake for fear of rolling backwards into the car behind. I recognise the same faithless flitting from one emotion to another, the paranoia, the feeling of being trapped and exposed as a fraud. My paranoia increased, anxiety replaced confidence, and I was unable to move the car in either direction out of danger. So, in desperation, I switched off the engine, got out and calmly walked the few yards up the hill, then turned the first corner and ran. I ran away leaving that stolen vehicle blocking the road, laughing with joy and the daring of it all.

Those were the days when the innocence of adventure could be folded and refolded into even greater adventures and, like the childish telling of lies, be just as easily forgotten; when the seriousness of my intent was not compelled by rational thought but rested upon the simple choice of 'yes' or 'no'.

But there I was again, more experienced but obviously still none the wiser, with my adventures unfolding under misguided ambition and the false security of darkness.

Suddenly I was blasted awake by a cacophony of car horns sounding off behind me. I struggled to pull myself together and miraculously I could see again. The road ahead was clear now but through the rear-view mirror I could see a column of early morning commuters snarling like a pack of wild dogs, straining at the leash. And way up ahead the traffic lights were still on red . . . or had they changed and cycled back round again whilst I slept?

Then I was through the lights and picking up speed, but it felt as though I was still half asleep and going through the motions on autopilot. My movements seemed locked in slow motion, functioning seconds later than instructed. I was driving through a sort of dreamscape with my thoughts concentrated like a microchip with all the collected information printed on the insides of my eye-lids. I could see nothing other than the events panning out in my mind. So I was concentrating real hard now to keep my eyes open, but I was also aware that some parts of my brain were beginning to short circuit and burn out, and that pretty soon, if I wasn't careful, my thinking process would shut down completely.

Sometimes you don't realise you've entered the twilight zone until some really weird event suddenly explodes around you. It could be a small thing, a minute contradiction, but one that mocks your present reality; that pulls and stretches your sanity, stretching it until it becomes a thin thread, until it threatens to snap. Then you see yourself like you're experiencing some kind of out of body phenomenon, reacting to this unbelievable situation with such an intensity that you are inclined to believe it. That this aberration, this raving disorder of the mind, might, at the end of it all, be the real thing.

The twilight zone is a never ending spiral of events; an absurd proposition of fact contrary to reason or common sense. It is a visual fallacy that leaves you stumbling around in the half light, blindly gathering up your fears as you go, and trying to focus some attention on that other reality. I thought I was in control. I had it all sussed out but, inevitably, I discovered that sleep demands a respect all of its own and is not something to mess with.

So instead of winging that sixteenth to the other side of town I switched off the telephone, punched a tape into the car cassette, and waited for the cool reassuring sound of U2 to confirm my new mood. What I needed was a bed, any bed.

Conversation

Ellie's apartment, in the early evening

Two friends, Lance and April, are sitting at a coffee table in a flat in the Manningham area of Bradford. They're waiting for Ellie, Lance's girlfriend, to return home with the heroin she's gone out to score.

APRIL: I don't even bother to go out these days unless I'm coming here or I'm out on the rampage collecting my debts.

LANCE: Yeah? I should join you one of these days. We're owed loads of money too.

APRIL: You should've seen me last night grab hold of that fuckin' Sadie. She tried to escape, jumped into a taxi and locked all the doors. But it stopped at the traffic lights so I dived in and got her out. The driver's going, 'Aaahhh!' I said: 'Fuck you,' and dragged her right out.

LANCE: She owes us too but she's always got an excuse for not paying. This time it's: 'I'm getting hassle on the Beat so I haven't been working.'

APRIL: Fuck off! She was out there last night. What does she owe you?

LANCE: Well, it's only £35, but the thing is it was £20 to begin with, then she claimed she got locked up for a couple of nights. She came and borrowed some more and we haven't seen her since.

APRIL: Oh yeah, she's full of that, isn't she? The latest one I'm getting is: 'But it's only £15 –'

LANCE: So why doesn't she pay up then?

APRIL: Exactly! She says she was burgled so she can't pay me now. But I remember her telling Mo about that burglary ages ago.

LANCE: She's been burgled about 15 times now, hasn't she? Or so she claims.

APRIL: [*Raising her voice*] Burgled? Have you seen the fuckin' state of her house? There's nothing in it. Just the baby on the settee, that's all. Little Jesse sitting there on a pile of shitty nappies.

LANCE: [*Laughing*] Fuckin' amazing, isn't it?

The door bell rings.

APRIL: Was that the buzzer? I'm sure I heard the buzzer.

She leaps out of her seat towards the door, hoping that it might be Ellie, but returns with Melony following close behind.

7

It's only Mel. She wants a wrap, on credit. Can you sort it?

April returns to her place at the coffee table and lights herself a cigarette.

LANCE: We've only got a touch left, Mel. Ellie's gone out to score some more, she'll be back soon. Why don't you wait?

APRIL: Yo!, Mel. What time shall I call on you tonight?

Melony takes a seat in a corner of the room, instead of joining them at the coffee table, and tries her best to avoid April's direct gaze.

MELONY: I don't know. You're best speaking to *him* [*referring to her boyfriend*]. He thinks you're being funny.

APRIL: [*Provocatively blows cigarette smoke in Melony's direction*] How am I being funny? All I want is my fuckin' money. How 'funny' is that when all I've done is ask for it?

MELONY: [*Defensively*] Well that's what he thinks, anyway.

APRIL: He's the 'funny' one. Just 'cause I called him a cunt for calling the police, and he *is* too.

Lance, sensing the tension, jumps to his feet and stands between the two girls.

LANCE: [*To both women*] Oh no you don't. You're not fighting in here!

CONVERSATION

APRIL: [*Demolishes her cigarette in the ashtray with a great exaggerated action*] Exactly! All I want is the time to come and get my money, that's all. It'll save me having to run around – and all *this* shit!

MELONY: [*Completely cowed*] April, if I had the money myself I'd give it to you just to save the hassle. I'm sick of being in the middle.

APRIL: I don't care, Mel. I haven't got two pennies to rub together and everybody's going: 'It's only this, it's only that . . .' But no one's got it to pay me, have they?

MELONY: Yeah, but because you came yesterday, out of the blue like that, and the way you spoke to him –

APRIL: [*Loudly interrupting*] I WAS ANNOYED! He wouldn't come to the fuckin' window. He always speaks through you. He should come and talk to me himself.

MELONY: [*Finally giving in*] Yeah, you're right. I'm sorry.

APRIL: Right. So who's being funny, then?

MELONY: Maybe he's –

APRIL: [*Interrupting again*] Maybe nothing! I'm not gonna argue about it. I shouldn't have to go running around for my money. He should've brought it to me.

MELONY: I'll get it for you myself if he hasn't got it.

Lance, realising that he's being ignored, sits back down again and glues his eyes to the TV set, which has a picture but no sound.

9

APRIL: Yeah, that's better. I've got nothing; that's why I want it. I think I'll go and call on that fuckin' Maureen as well, she owes me too. And what about Sadie, have you seen her out there, Mel?

MELONY: I saw her last night. She starts work early now. Well before me, anyway.

In an attempt to placate Melony, Lance gives her his very last bit of heroin. He's expecting Ellie to return home any minute now with more heroin and doesn't want her to walk in on a row.

LANCE: [*Handing over a small square of tin foil*] There you go, Mel. I've squeezed it out for you. It's not much but it's better than nothing. Just give us a buzz tomorrow and if no one answers you can shove the money under the door, okay?

Melony takes the wrap of heroin with a painful look of gratitude and shoves it down her cleavage. She side-steps her way around to the front door, still staying well out of April's line of vision.

MELONY: [*To Lance*] Thanks love. I really appreciate this. I won't let you down.

APRIL: [*To no one in particular*] I'm going for a mooch about, see if I can find anyone out there.

MELONY: [*To April, feigning surprise*] Are you going? I'll walk with you then.

LANCE: I'll walk with you too. I'm gonna phone my mum and tell her I'm in shit street: 'I can't afford to buy any more drugs mummy. Can I have a loan?'

APRIL: What about Ellie, how's she gonna get in?

LANCE: Don't worry about it, she's got her own keys.

MELONY: Lance, has Ellie got any spare Durex? I know she gets them free from that needle exchange, doesn't she? They're dead expensive you know, £1 odd, for a packet of three. That's expensive when you need dozens every night like I do.

APRIL: [*Pissed off again*] Yeah, you've got money for them, haven't you? Why don't you get down to the exchange and get some yourself. What's wrong with you?

Everybody gets up to leave: Melony home to smoke her wrap; April to chase up her debts; Lance to phone his mother.

Ellie

As far as I know, a junkie's body is completely different to other people's. Our blood cells don't just need food and water, iron, zinc and all those other minerals, we also need heroin. A simple way to prove this is to look at people who're withdrawing from barbiturates or tranquillisers. The withdrawals are so severe they can die from fits or from not getting the drugs their cells have come to depend on. Just like you starve to death without food, they can also die without their tranquillisers. That's one of the reasons why doctors shouldn't suddenly stop prescriptions. But then they get on to this power trip and make you suffer for something you're supposed to have done wrong. They're pathetic, abusing their powers like that, 'cause it really can lead to someone's death.

I remember once I got nicked for something or other and I was withdrawing in the police cells. They sent a doctor in to see me but he just turned round and said: 'People don't die from withdrawals, they die from buying heroin.' There was this kid who'd OD'd on some gear that I'd been charged with supplying and what the doctor meant was that kid had died because of me. His attitude was, 'Tough shit, lady. I don't care that you're withdrawing, there's somebody dead because of you.' What a bastard! I mean, what happened to 'Innocent until proved guilty'?

I'm in the cells being questioned about that kid and he's coming down on me for being a junkie. He was blaming me for that guy's death and refusing to give me medication, as if I *was* guilty simply because he'd decided it.

Okay, so maybe he wasn't speaking from a legal point of view. Being a doctor he was probably talking ethics: that all of us, drug dealers and drug addicts, were guilty of that guy's death. But I wasn't dealing with that, all I was interested in was getting something for my withdrawals. He said, 'Go back to your cell, there's nothing wrong with you. All you need is food.' That's exactly what I mean. As far as they're concerned all we need is food and water. But I know they're wrong because we need heroin too.

Lanre: Aesthetics and Mechanics

It doesn't take genius or any specialist inside knowledge to be a drug dealer. In fact it's quite simple really, you just learn as you go. You buy, you chop, you mix, you measure, bag and sell. Simple as that. It's a business like any other business, dependent upon common sense and luck.

But dealing crack cocaine, in particular, can be a tricky business and often requires more than a simple dose of good fortune. In addition to its illegality, the attention it attracts from the police and other drug dealers, the powerful and dramatic effects of the product itself can often seduce the dealer even more than the proceeds of its wealth. The sweetness of Charlie's 'rush' can be even greater than its re-sale value. Therefore a good dealer ought to know at least some detail about the effects cocaine has upon their punter's psyche; they should also recognise their own limitations if they're to hustle the product successfully.

Cocaine is the Top Gun of the drugs market and as such commands an obscene amount of respect. If you have coke you have status, you have power; you are somebody to be reckoned with. Its popularity as a good-time drug is determined by its power to stimulate pleasure and generate immense wealth, which far outweighs the dangers of hustling a commodity which, at today's prices, is more costly than gold.

Its profit margins are enormous and significantly overshadow regular street drugs such as cannabis, amphetamine, and even the modern phenomenon ecstasy. On the street, where top-grade skunk weed can be bought for anything up to £200 an ounce, cocaine commands a price in excess of £1,000.

But street coke hardly ever comes pure unless it's bought in bulk (by that I mean by the boat load) and even then there are no guarantees.

Coca paste – cultivated coca leaves processed on jungle farms in the wilds of Bolivia and Peru – is exported to Colombian laboratories where it is refined and converted to cocaine hydrochloride then smuggled north to the USA. By the time it leaves America and reaches these shores your average wrap of coke, bought on the street, has gone through so many hands you're lucky if what you're snorting or free-basing contains any cocaine at all.

Everybody 'steps' on their product before selling it on. Even a 200 per cent cut is not unheard of. So long as the punter gets a numbed nose or a crackling pipe they're usually satisfied. But a good dealer will cut their product according to their punter's taste. They know from experience that there are very few people who know anything about cocaine and even less who've ever tasted pure.

So cocaine is now a seller's market where a dealer can 'step' on his, already cut, product as much as he wants to because there are always enough suckers out there to buy up grams of crack cocaine as fast as the dealer can put them out.

In his introduction to Robert Sabbag's *Snowblind*, Howard Marks, the legendary cannabis smuggler confirms that 'scamming [hustling] is no more than a combination of waiting and winging it, preceded by the most labyrinthine of plans, fall backs, and security procedures . . .'

Since the introduction of crack cocaine, Bradford's Front Line has become a place for the opportunist. It is a hustler's market, a druggies' bazaar, where anything goes and everything comes and goes. To some local residents it is already the epitome of hell on earth.

Whilst the more serious hustler is a businessman (albeit illegal) and wouldn't be seen dead hanging around the Front Line, the gathering herd of opportunists come from far and wide to ply their trade. They present themselves as the main attraction and approach their work as tough guys rather than smart; they seem not to understand the need for planning or even security procedures.

So the newly arrived drug dealer has got the product in and the cash is flowing, All he needs now is a place to stash it all. But banking it is out. He knows only suckers fall for that one. He's not having a stranger, some fuckin' white-collar stiff, getting his greasy hands all over his wad. No man! He knows exactly where his little bundle is going – straight under the bed. Stashed away under his mattress, nice and snug where no fucker will find it!

Meanwhile the junkies and crack heads don't give a fuck. All they have to do is follow their noses. They know exactly where and how to sniff out the drugs. Every hour of every day is spent working out how to score the next fix, where to find the next rock. It's like a necklace of beads with one bead, one day, one event being threaded on at a time until their lives are fully strung out.

Although the police, drug enforcement agencies, and customs officers make a big show of fighting this so called 'drugs war', the average cop on the beat has no real interest in eradicating drugs off the street, whether they be class 'A' or any other category. Since their promotion is more easily gained via the number of arrests they make they much prefer to detain a number of individuals rather than participate in one big operation. They're in the business of detention rather than prevention, so why should they make any attempt at cleaning up the streets when it is via that same drugs war that they seek to promote themselves.

So stashing away your drugs and keeping the area in which you operate as clean as possible is everything when you're dealing off the street. Having to be lucky *ALL* the time, whereas the police only have to be lucky once, means exactly that. You cannot afford to be slack in this routine. It is perhaps the single most important thing that will keep you out of jail.

Lance

My parents have known about my drug problem since I was nineteen years old. My old man caught me shooting up in the house one Christmas while the family was spending the holiday with relatives in Kent. We were supposed to stay for a week but I'd run short of heroin and needed to score, so I made up this really pathetic excuse and split back home.

Once I was home I realised that I had the house to myself, since the rest of the family weren't due home for a couple of days, so I invited a few friends round. I sorted myself out with a dig then washed out my works and put them down by the kitchen sink. Suddenly a car pulled up outside and through the window I saw my parents coming up the drive. I don't think they were expecting anything really but they were a bit suspicious that *something* was going on. I freaked out when I saw them and screamed at my mates to clear up. My parents were back!

One of my friends threw her coat over the table and everyone hauled the gear, all the works and stuff, into this massive bundle then, just as my parents came in, we all rushed out saying we were going down the pub. But

I remembered that I'd left my works by the sink, so I had to go back into the house, pretending that I wanted a drink of water – and this is after I've just said that I'm going down to the pub!

I went over to the sink and tried to slide the syringe up my sleeve but my mother sussed me and asked what I had in my hand. Obviously I pretended I didn't know what she was talking about but she'd already seen the syringe lying there, so that was it; I was busted.

I was surprised they didn't kick off – they really were quite lenient. They already had an idea that I was using, anyway, but I said it was just a bit of speed. 'I've only done it a couple of times, mum, it won't happen again.' I was, like, taken aback 'cause they were pretty easy going about it all. Within ten minutes they were okay and I was out the door.

At that time I was living in a flat in Worthing, so I went back to my place then off to the pub. That evening we were due to go up to London to score but I was suspicious that my parents were on to me. In the flat there was loads of stuff like works, dope, scales, you know, just lying around, so at my parents' house I hid my keys in my bedroom, behind a wardrobe, and went off to London. When I came back they were both sitting in the front room with the scales, box of works, the whole lot. They'd searched my bedroom, found the keys, gone over to my flat, about twenty miles away, got all the stuff, took it back to their own house and laid it out for me. I'd walked straight into that one and now it was showdown time. So that first one was really the calm before the storm. And what a fuckin' storm it was.

The thing is, I'd just got back from London with an ounce of gear in my pocket, so I was dying for a hit. All I wanted them to do was get it over with and shut up so I could go upstairs and have my hit. That's all I cared about. They didn't catch me then but they have caught me a couple of times before, actually digging gear.

I used to work in Petworth, my dad was working at the college and my mum went off to work early. On this particular day I was waiting for my dad to go so I could have a hit before I went to work but he was waiting for me to get out of the house, just to make sure that I went. So we were sort of stalling each other but eventually we both went out. I just went round the block on my motor bike, parked it up around the back of the house, and went in through the front door. For some reason I put the little latch chain on the front door and went upstairs.

So I've got my hit together and was just about to crank it up when I heard this almighty crash, as my old man booted the front door in and came belting up the stairs. He'd come back home on the pretext that he'd left something behind but I think he had an idea of what was going on. All I could think about was *Just get the gear in, get it in*. So I carried on pushing the gear in as he came into the room and he just came up to me and smacked me in the face. I still had the works in my arm when he walked out again. He was so furious. But I admit I had put them through quite a lot of shit by this time. And it had all been building up since that first time on Christmas Day.

Conversation

Ellie's apartment, in the evening

It's evening and, after phoning his parents, Lance returns home in a foul mood. He's pleased to see that Ellie has returned from scoring since he's looking for a shoulder to cry on. But the presence of April sitting in his front room irritates him even further.

Ellie, a woman in her early thirties, with the gaunt, under-nourished appearance which is the result of seventeen years of heroin abuse, is in the room with a small cosmetics bag on the coffee table. She opens the bag, takes out a spoon, a couple of syringes, needles, etc, and lays them on the table. Then from the gusset of her leggings she pulls out a small bag of heroin and lays that on the table next to her paraphernalia. She sits down and begins to prepare a dig for herself and Lance, but his dramatic entrance and visible upset startle her to her feet.

ELLIE: Lance, are you alright?

LANCE: No!

ELLIE: Why what's up, what's the matter?

LANCE: [*Pacing the room*] Well, you know, my old man . . . It happens every time I talk to him. He's so narrow minded. He's retired at fifty-seven years old and d'you know what he's so fuckin' bitter about? The fact that all his life my mother has earned more money than him. He's like . . . Oh shit . . . I don't wanna bitch about my old man.

Lance stops pacing the room and stands with his shoulders slumped, staring out of the window. He continues the conversation with his face turned away from Ellie.

I should be like him, I suppose. Christ, what does he want from me?

He steps away from the window and walks over to Ellie on the other side of the room. But, just at the last minute, he turns his back on her, kicks over a dining chair, then storms out of the room. Ellie follows him out and from the hallway his complaints can be heard.

What the fuck is she still doing here? I thought she'd gone.

ELLIE: [*Very gently*] Oh, don't worry about her. What's your dad been saying?

LANCE: Oh, just leave it, babes.

After a short silence where the two hug and reconcile, they both wander back into the living room.

LANCE: [*To Ellie, deliberately ignoring April*] So, how did it go then, everything okay?

ELLIE: Yeah, no problem. He was already there waiting for me.

APRIL: Lance, are we still getting that sixteenth tomorrow?

ELLIE: Who from, B.Jay? Do you mean the same stuff as this?

LANCE: [*Still ignoring April*] Yeah. If the price is right. He said he'll give us a tester.

APRIL: No, fuck B.Jay, he's full of shit.

ELLIE: Yeah, I know. But this is all the same gear and it's supposed to be really good.

APRIL: He won't give us fuck all. He's a bullshitter. He's just into ripping people off. Hanging round us all the time and getting freebies.

Lance gives April a knowing look, suggesting it's the same game that she's playing.

LANCE: He sat here once for four hours, waiting to ask Ellie for a turn on. I mean we were all over each other, practically screwing on the sofa, trying to get rid of him, you know, but he just sat there!

APRIL: Why didn't you tell him to fuck off?

LANCE: Yeah, I know, but it doesn't work. And even then, when he's ready, he just goes and sits at someone else's house.

APRIL: [*To Ellie*] Didn't he used to hang out with Anwar?

ELLIE: Yeah. They got into this guy called Frank who was in that half-way house down the road. He had a couple of grand in the bank so they helped him spend it all on smack. They got him on a right habit.

APRIL: Fuckin' bang out of order. They're like fuckin' leeches, all of them.

LANCE: That Frank was in Lynfield Mount, wasn't he? He was into gear for ages but he gave it up. Then they got into him and fucked him up good style. They've dumped him now, haven't they? Now that he's stone broke.

APRIL: [*Pointing to the heroin Ellie is cooking up*] Jesus Christ! Look how much Ellie's putting into that spoon, that's enough to knock an elephant over!

ELLIE: We used to do a lot more than this, you know.

APRIL: [*Seeing the opportunity that she's been waiting for, April seizes her chance*] Can you do me a £10 wrap 'til tomorrow?

Lance, knowing that this was coming, storms out of the room again in protest.

ELLIE: [*Ignoring Lance*] Shit, why does everyone always hassle me for it?

APRIL: [*Deliberately changing the subject*] D'you remember that time when Nicky turned up from Manchester wanting a £10 wrap on tick? He came all that way in a taxi without any money, and still wanted credit 'cause he was withdrawing.

ELLIE: Yeah, he'd even shit himself before he got here. Lance has gone down to see what he wants and he's shouting up: 'Look, I'm sick, I've shit myself too.' At quarter to nine in the morning. Lance is waiting to take Deborah to school. We got him into the flat so the neighbours wouldn't hear and he actually came and sat on my bed. 'Look, I've shit myself,' he says. He's even trying to show it to me. I'm telling him to fuck off out of my house but he keeps telling me how poorly he is. But I was withdrawing too, I was sweating like a pig. I had gear under the pillow and he says: 'What're you doing with gear, why don't you have a dig?' But I couldn't afford to, I had to sell it.

APRIL: Sometimes I've had to do that. I've been withdrawing and got smack in my pocket but I can't smoke any 'cause I've given out so much credit that I can't afford to touch anymore.

ELLIE: We got rid of Nicky in the end. Lance told him to leave his jacket behind to cover the wrap, then fuck off.

APRIL: I wouldn't have let him in. If he'd said that in front of my kid he'd have been out that fuckin' door.

Lance returns to the room in a more cheerful mood and is ready to rejoin the conversation.

LANCE: [*To April*] I found it really hard not to smack him one.

APRIL: What about when he had that punter downstairs?

ELLIE: Oh shit, yeah!

25

LANCE: He buzzed us from downstairs and said in that girlie voice of his, 'It's me, Nicky.' So I let him in. After about ten minutes he still hasn't come up so I went downstairs to see what'd happened to him. I opened the doors in the hallway, switched on the lights, and he's only going gobble, gobble, gobble, on some bloke down there.

ELLIE: He's doing a fuckin' punter in our passageway. Then he gets the money and comes running back upstairs to buy a wrap off us.

APRIL: He's fuckin' amazing, isn't he?

ELLIE: And this is all in the same week that he's told us about shitting himself. I must be a real sucker!

Having prepared the digs for herself and Lance, Ellie finally gives April the heroin she asked for.

APRIL: Thanks Ellie, that's a really nice wrap that. I just can't get over the amount you two use. That'd be enough to kill me three times over.

ELLIE: We don't even get a hit off it anymore. It's just enough to see us right.

APRIL: I'm looking at mine and thinking, 'Fuckin' hell, they don't feel it!' Are you joking?

LANCE: It's not what the fix looks like, that's just liquid, it's the amount of opiate in it that counts.

APRIL: [*Referring to her own dig*] I might as well do this then?

ELLIE: Yeah, 'course you can, if you get yourself a clean spoon.

APRIL: I'm easy. Do you wanna cook this for me? I was gonna say you can put this through the same as yours. I'm not really bothered. Is that clean water there, Ellie?

ELLIE: Yeah. You'll need to boil it in a spoon though, but it is clean. Anyway, AIDS is such a weak –

APRIL: [*Interrupting*] I don't give a fuck what I die of to be quite honest.

ELLIE: Aw, leave it out, April!

APRIL: No, no. What I'm saying is if I did have AIDS it wouldn't be like –

ELLIE: [*Interrupting*] How can you say that?

APRIL: I'm just saying that I'm not bothered what I die of, that's all.

ELLIE: Yeah, but you've got to be so careful. It's like suicide, isn't it?

APRIL: What I'm saying is, if I did have AIDS it wouldn't bother me. Obviously I don't wanna catch it but it's no different from cancer. You know what I'm saying? At the end of the day there's still no cure for cancer so why is AIDS different?

LANCE: I'll tell you what does annoy me. You know how we're always giving away needles and things? The other day I was talking to the pharmacist when I went to pick up my script and he said that it's illegal for us to give them away.

APRIL: Yeah, but at the end of the day, Lance, it's better to do that than let people share.

LANCE: I know. Five years ago it was really hard to find them. When I used to live in Chichester I had to go all the way to Brighton for them. I told the chemist that sometimes we get friends coming round who haven't got any clean works, so we give them some. What's wrong with that?

APRIL: Nothing! What about that time we were round at Nicky's? They were picking them up off the floor! Okay, so they boiled them, but they still came off the floor.

ELLIE: Yeah, right. They had the stuff in this plastic thing and it had fag ash and dirt and everything in it. D'you remember that? I mean, it was grey not white!

APRIL: I bet they've got diseases and all sorts over there.

ELLIE: It wouldn't surprise me if they have. They even use each other's works.

APRIL: This isn't cool enough, is it? I'll run it under the tap for a bit. Lance, could you get me a hit straight off? I keep missing the vein.

LANCE: Ellie's better at it than me, to tell you the truth.

APRIL: Oh, right, yeah, she's the boss. Dr Oops!

ELLIE: One time Nicky came round and he was so sick

that he stuck the works in his arm and just squirted the whole lot in. Then he's going, 'Ow, ow, ow. Can I have another one 'cause I've just put that one under?' And then he said, 'But I haven't got any money, though.' The fuckin' cheek of it. I don't know how they manage to dig anything. Fuckin' hell. He went down in the cellar one day and asked me to fix him in his groin. There's absolutely no way I'd stick a needle in someone else's groin. I just couldn't do it. So I left him down there. Twenty minutes later I went back down and he was sat with his leg stuck up in the air. He'd stuck the needle in his thigh, sucked the blood up into the barrel, thought it was a funny colour and just whacked it in. He'd got the artery! His fuckin' leg had blown right up. It was unbelievable.

APRIL: I remember them once having a dirty hit, Nicky and Tamsin. We were running around getting them gear, trying to make them better. But I think they were fannying us, though, 'cause Tamsin was on top of Nicky by the time we got there.

LANCE: There really is no need for it. If you think about the amount of effort you put into getting the gear, the amount of money you spend. I mean, ten 1mm syringes at £1.80 . . . It really isn't necessary to use them more than once. That's why the needle exchange is so good. You don't even have to be registered.

APRIL: Yeah, but you've got to take your card. You can't just get them for nothing.

LANCE: No you don't, you don't need a card. Basically,

if you need anything you can just walk into any chemist that does the needle exchange and get them for free. You don't need to give your name, address, or any ID. You just join the exchange. It's that simple.

APRIL: I never refuse people needles, I gave B.Jay a handful the other day.

LANCE: I've talked to Mr Levin, you know, the pharmacist on Oak Lane, about why he doesn't do the exchange. We ended up arguing. He said he doesn't do it because there's no money in it for him. He uses that age old argument about not encouraging drug abuse. But he's prepared to accept junkies on his books and hand out Methadone. There's money in that for him, isn't there!

Lanre: The Hall of Mirrors

I was out of town sitting naked in the middle of someone's living room floor staring at yet another empty crack pipe. The girl sitting next to me was also naked except for this flimsy black top, and had just smoked the last rock. It was about four fifteen in the morning. We'd been piping and fooling around with each other most of the night, then my balls began to ache . . .

The potential had been that good, yet somehow I felt cheated; like I'd been missing the point and that the real action had been taking place somewhere else. Then she started crawling about on her hands and knees, searching the floor, hoping to find another rock, another crumb; looking for the buzz and that breathless rush to her head again, but I was thinking to myself that I had to get that girl away from the pipe and into something else; I had to salvage what I could from that night before the passion was lost completely and I was left out in the cold again. Then I remembered the two grams of pure crystal cocaine I had stashed somewhere in the lining of my jacket – two grams of mother of pearl!

If I can just get her to try a little, I thought. *Snort up a couple of lines instead of blasting it away on that fuckin' pipe, then maybe she'll appreciate its real power. Maybe then, as it percolates through her body and tickles her sex, she'll remember the real purpose of us being here.* But it was like she didn't want to know as I began chopping up the crystals and forming them into lines. She was wired and picking at a dry spot in the carpet, fussing over a tiny spec of white and hoping against hope that she'd found another chip of rock.

I took a £20 note from the pile of money strewn across the floor and rolled it into a tight tube. Then carefully, ever so carefully, leaned over the cocaine and sniffed up two lines, one in each nostril.

B-E-A-U-T-I-F-U-L!

The powder immediately hit the back of my throat, numbing it completely. Seconds later the rush and an overwhelming sense of euphoria.

She was still on her hands and knees when I handed her the tooter, with her cute little bum stuck up in the air, and her naked sex flashing in the lamplight. I wasn't sure whether the expression on her face was due to that lucky find in the carpet or simply wishful thinking on my part. But then suddenly she was up on her feet and padding across the floor, homing in on the cocaine like a bitch-junkie on remote control, sniffing and fumbling and trying to get all the drug down at one time. And I was restraining her, taking up a position from behind and gently pulling her back by the hips, trying to slow her down. I could feel skin against skin rubbing up a gentle friction, my dick rising, growing hard and restless, eager for the action. But her liquid fast movements were too quick for me as she blurred over everything and anything in her desperate haste to get at the hit. Then WHAM! Just like that she botched it. JESUS FUCKIN' CHRIST! She was so greedy and impatient she blew all my precious hoard on to the floor and I was left with my dick in my hand, having to deal with the anti-climax.

But that girl was something else. A natural blonde with soft, sensual lips and that virginal fresh look of an innocent child. A regular Lolita . . . We weren't good friends, though. I didn't even know her name. She was just some place I could rest my head and chill out when the anxieties of the day became intolerable; somewhere to sleep without the unnecessary drama of sex and drugs. Well that was the intention. Only when I turned up on her doorstep with a pocket full of crack, she appeared to be so overjoyed to see me that any notion I had of getting some sleep that night was instantly lost.

I gave her a rock as a thank you for letting me stay. She immediately broke it in two and blasted off one half right there in the hallway almost before I'd shut the front door behind me. Then she was in the living room stripping off her clothes and blazing the other half. I didn't really understand what the nudity was about but I didn't care! From where I was standing she looked pretty good, turning herself on with that stone. So I threw her another one whilst simultaneously throwing off my own clothes as fast as I could. I intended to give that girl the monster fuck of her young life but she was way ahead of me, right down to that last rock.

We drugged ourselves stupid that night and spent hours squelching over the floor, slipping and sliding in and out of each other's juices. I tried to take her a thousand different ways, a thousand times over, but it was to no avail . . . Lolita didn't fuck. Well not with me anyway.

She was only in it for the drugs and offered me nothing in return other than what was already mine, '. . . another pipe?'

Then, when the drugs had finished, the party was over, and the harsh reality of daylight came crashing in through the window, she turned her back on me and didn't want to know. She pulled on her knickers, opened the window blinds and scurried off somewhere else. Maybe to someone else. Just like that . . . another back-handed smack in the mouth.

Suddenly I was tired again, but I was so fuckin' angry. I could feel the rage snaking around my insides, tormenting me, like I'd been suckered and should've known better, like I should've seen it coming. I mean, Christ, she'd practically advertised her intent from the start. Only the drugs and all those sugar-coated suggestions of something special, something even more weird and wonderful, must've taken my mind away. And like some dippy cartoon character, I'd leapt straight in without even a second thought. Tragic.

I stood there in the middle of the room staring at the spot she'd just vacated, and at the dozens of empty cocaine wraps trashed on the floor and that fuckin' pipe spilling ash and nasty rancid water into the carpet. And I could feel this strange, bitter desire to take back everything I'd shared with her that night, to efface all traces of laughter and excitement. I wanted to deny her the power she had over me. It was like the bitch had hijacked my mind because I just couldn't think straight.

Pure blinding rage coursed through my veins, boiling up my blood and, I swear to God, if I'd had something in my hands . . . My mind flashed an image of me shooting her in the head. I imagined the bullet spinning off into the distance slow-motion style, as her head snapped back off her shoulders, an expression of shock frozen on her face, with blood squirting up the wall like a fantail. But I knew I was only tripping . . . Just pride and drugs messing with my head again, that's all, daring me to make an even bigger fool of myself. It was all bullshit, anyway. Even as I savoured the wickedness of my feelings towards her I knew, in my heart, that the wickedness was really directed at myself. The fault was my own.

Gathering my clothes up off the floor, I noticed the spot where she'd blown my cocaine away and flinched again, before making my way through to the bathroom. I ran the wash basin full of cold water then plunged my head in there, hoping that would help, somehow, to calm me down before I hit the streets again. But the events of the previous night kept replaying themselves in my mind, over and over again, like some third rate horror movie threatening to fuck me up altogether. I was wired and stressed out like Freddie Kruger and could've done with a rock to lift my spirits. But that would've been disastrous. Besides, I had nothing left anyway, that bitch had cleaned me out.

It was impossible to ascertain just how much crack we had blazed away that night, just as it was impossible to recoup the loss. I hadn't sold a single rock, not one fuckin' stone, and neither had I got any sleep!

But what alarmed me wasn't the fact that I'd allowed that scheming little junkie to toss me off like that, nor was it my lack of money and cocaine. No, what really bugged me was my unrelenting desire to smoke the damn stuff. And perhaps even worse was what appeared to be my inability to do anything about it. The truth of the matter was that the events of that night were becoming all too common. I realised that more and more frequently I'd been losing myself in lengthy bingeing sessions, emerging hours, sometimes days, later with no drugs, no money, no nothing. Sometimes I'd be so pissed off that the only way to lift myself up again was to get high. Then the bingeing would start all over again.

Eventually, after what seemed like hours, though surely it could only have been minutes, the cold water gently massaging my temples began to take effect. I straightened up and towelled myself dry in front of the mirror.

I was feeling better, as though somewhere in that jumble of mixed emotions a light had been switched on and, suddenly, I was aware of my fragility, my secret illness and need. I recognised that same old irresistible urge, the compulsion, the tension and yielding to that impulse, followed by depression and the compulsion once again. It was always at those moments of diminished power, when the odds appeared to be stacked up against me, that I felt at my worse. Yet this feeling was a kind of *déjà vu*, as I stood face to face with myself in a hall of mirrors; ducking and diving, shrinking away from the million images of myself reflected and refracted back through the glass. What I saw in that mirror was not the confident smiling face with a look of gentle understanding that I expected to see, but a wretchedness, an emotional discomposure that appeared fallible and ugly. I was confronted by an image of what I'd become, a reflection of myself as others saw me, highlighting the disparity between my external self and inner truth.

Maureen

I think if I was a wife I would much prefer my husband to go with prostitutes than have an affair. With a prostitute it's just straightforward, meaningless sex but if he was having an affair he could easily fall in love with the woman and she'd steal my man away. I wouldn't be able to handle it. That's why I don't go back home with married punters anymore.

The last punter who took me back to his house was married. He wanted straight sex and paid me £50. So we were sitting there talking, sort of getting to know each other, when suddenly his wife came home. He just flipped and told me to hide in the cupboard under the stairs. But I was freaked out myself and told him to fuck off. I wasn't going to hide from anyone, especially when I hadn't done anything, and I didn't know how long I was supposed to hide for. Anything could happen and I would've been hiding in that tiny cupboard like a divvy. So I just sat there waiting in the front room whilst he went into shock.

He wasn't bad looking for a punter but his wife was a big, fat, ugly thing, twice the size of him, and when she saw me in her house he tried to pass me off as the next door neighbour's niece. All I could do was nod in agreement but she wasn't having it and they ended up arguing. I could hear them in the kitchen shouting at each other, then she came back into the room and said, 'I know who you are. Tell me the truth, how long has this been going on?' I honestly thought she meant how long had we been fuckin' each other so I said, 'We haven't started yet.'

That must've really hurt because then she pointed to the packet of condoms on the coffee table and screamed so loud I thought she was going to hit me.

She was hysterical: 'I know you're having an affair with my husband. Tell me, how long has it been going on?'

I couldn't believe it. It was just so funny but in a way it wasn't. She really believed we were having an affair. All those times he was out kerb-crawling prostitutes she thought he'd been seeing another woman. I almost felt sorry for her and had to admit that I was a prostitute, but she didn't believe me. She thought I was covering up for him. I told her the truth and tried to make her understand but she wouldn't listen. She just couldn't get off that stupid idea that I was the 'other woman', so the only thing I could do to prove it was to take her up to the beat. She was pretty shocked. I could see it in her eyes as it dawned on her. I even got a policeman, a vice cop, to identify me. Her husband was wriggling and squirming in the back seat, trying to hide, but she just told him to shut up and sit still. Finally she believed me and apologised. Then she turned around and started beating up her husband. But all that time had cost me money so I charged them another £50 and left them to it.

I've seen him again since then but there was no way I was going back to that house. He said she'd allowed him to come and see me again because she was pregnant and she preferred him to be with me, a prostitute, than have an affair.

Sadie
(Lanre's Voice)

Pale-faced Sadie with the mournful eyes, swinging down Manningham Lane, hand in hand with a new boyfriend. All dressed up like a chilli pepper, she's wearing red Adidas tracksuit bottoms and a white top, stained pink in the washing machine.

Her dark hair, as usual, is a thick tangled mess. But there's something about its bounce, the way it blows freely in the wind . . . Something that makes my blood boil. She *must* have some money, otherwise what the fuck is she doing out at this time in the morning and looking so damn pleased with herself, too?

From where I'm parked, outside the Mayflower Club, I can see the two of them are having themselves a fine time, like a couple of jabbering love birds. She's skipping along, her feet barely touching the ground, laughing and joking at something he's said, openly and without a care in the world. I can feel my head pounding as anger rises like bile from the pit of my stomach, so forcefully that any sense of reason is instantly lost. Tightening my grip on the steering wheel I make a violent U-turn, screeching to a stop just inches away from her kneecaps. Then, glowering at the boyfriend, I bundle her in to the back for a search.

She kicks and screams like a fat pig but I don't give a fuck. She owes me money and I want it. Simple. Then I rifle through her pockets. She tries to get there before me but a sharp slap in the mouth soon puts a stop to that. Her head slams backwards, eyes wide open, and before she has time to register the shock, I'm ready to give her another one. But then she goes all limp and docile on me. She lifts up her top to show me that she's not hiding anything but I'm not impressed. I know she just wants out of this madness and back to the safety of her boyfriend, who's poised on the edge of the pavement doing all this macho stuff; trying to make himself look big but still not daring to make a move.

If looks could kill I'd be a dead man, but they can't and I know it. Passers-by observe the scene but no one interferes. Even the cab drivers ranked just a few yards away mind their own business.

This is an everyday occurrence in Manningham and they've seen it all before.

It's no big thing.

I grab hold of Sadie's top by the neck-line and yank it off completely, then the tracksuit bottoms, tights and knickers. And there she is, naked. Her whole body exposed: tits, belly, thighs, all merging together in one great expanse of flesh, like a mountain of jelly quivering under its own weight. Before I'm able to recoil away from this obscenity I'm hit by the smell.

A smell of unclean sex so rank and putrid that it works against me like some sort of defence system, smashing my senses to smithereens and destroying the impetus of my bully-boy tactics. Suddenly, my violence spent, I feel tired and exhausted.

I'm looking at Sadie and I mean *really* looking at her, as though I'm seeing her for the first time, sitting there in the back seat of my car with her tits and everything hanging out, without shame, not even bothering to cover herself. Just sitting there with a dull look of resignation in her eyes, as though something has been switched off from the inside.

She has no money, only an assortment of condoms and a £10 wrap of heroin stashed in the gusset of her knickers. And now I'm beginning to feel doubtful, wondering why am I doing this. Wondering how much more can be stripped away from this woman that she hasn't given up already? How much more violence can she endure? But this is weak. You start thinking like that, questioning and doubting yourself, letting the bastards into your skull and it's enough to fuck you up. You gotta keep it tight, don't give yourself away. But I just want out of here, as far away from her as possible. I wanna get away before my doubt turns into guilt. But I know the boyfriend is still out there watching me, taking it all in, so I have to keep up the act.

You know it's strange, even as we're sinking, slipping and sliding in our own bullshit, we still feel the need to preserve ourselves. We still look for something, any-thing, to hold on to. Something that restores our pride and stands us back up on our feet.

So I kick her out of the car and slam the door behind her, even before she's managed to dress herself properly. Then I'm gunning the motor away from there, my foot slammed down on the accelerator, skidding away, making a big show of it.

And I'm watching Sadie through the rear-view mirror spilling out on to the pavement. And I'm wishing to God that I'd never spotted her in the first place.

The Monk

April 1985 my mother was diagnosed with cancer and died three months later. When she got her first test results back from the hospital she made us all promise that we wouldn't talk about it. She said that if there was anything wrong she didn't want to know. So we brought her home on the pretext that she'd suffered a collapsed lung and nobody said a word.

Then one night she's lying in bed and it's like she's about to go. Suddenly it's time for our souls to be bared, for goodbyes to be said. She grabbed hold of my hand and looked me right in the eye, but before she could say anything I said, 'Hang on a minute, mum, I'm just going to the shop.' Then I ran out and didn't go back. Can you imagine that, '. . . just going to the shop!' It was the strangest thing. I knew my mother was dying and we had a lot to talk about, 'cause there wasn't gonna be another opportunity, but I just couldn't handle it. So I bottled out.

There *are* situations in life that I can wriggle out of, usually by lying, but when death arises it's non-manipulative. It's right there in your face and unavoid-able. For something to be so final like that is alien to me. There was no way to escape, I couldn't get around it, so I just blanked it out. And all that pretence about there being nothing wrong with my mother was good for me. I liked it because I didn't have to face up to anything. It became like *my* story then.

I mean, I *was* angry with her for putting me in such a position but, hey, what a good piece of ammunition for my arsenal. I could tell myself that I was to blame, it was all my fault. I was at a crisis point and I liked it because the pressure gave me an excuse to use even more drugs. It was like a great lump of self-hatred that I could throw at myself.

Obviously my mother's death had nothing to do with me. We all die at some point, don't we, so how the fuck could it have been my fault? But times change . . . and I still need the guilt. It's like self-flagellation. You know what I mean? I still find ways of using the guilt to shut *him* up inside my head: the real me, the Monk who's not on drugs. I mean, if I couldn't even sit down and face up to my mother's death then what chance have I got of facing up to my drug problem?

Conversation

Ellie's apartment, in the afternoon

Ellie and her friend Maureen, who's managed to get time out from her boyfriend, are sitting in Ellie's living room catching up on the gossip.

MAUREEN: Yo! Yo! This is my bloke I was telling you about. You know, my man. The one who stuck that great lump of rock in his ear!

ELLIE: What, you mean crack?

MAUREEN: [*Laughing*] Yeah. Fuckin' dickhead. He got nervous 'cause the Old Bill were sniffing around so he tried to hide it in his ear – of all places! We spent ages trying to dig it out. It was massive. We'd just scored a rock off Dizzy and the police saw us coming out of his house, so Dave thought they were on to us. I mean they were right behind us on the steps, giving us the eye.

ELLIE: Wasn't it Dizzy's house where that kid nearly got killed?

MAUREEN: Yeah. It was *me* who saw Sadie take him to the house for business. That was about 10 o'clock. She must've only had half-an-hour to get him upstairs and rip him off, which is what probably happened. They found him outside his own house at ten-thirty. Dizzy reckons it had nothing to do with them but all their stuff was taken by the forensics, so they haven't got off with it yet. When they were bailed out, Sadie told me they'd got the Monk for it. No one else has said anything yet so it still hasn't been confirmed. But I think Dizzy did it. His banister, going up to the flat, is wobbling all over the place and straightaway I said, 'Someone must've thrown the kid over the banister and broken his neck.' The banister was a bit dodgy before but now it's all over the place. Yeah, I think Dizzy and Sadie are in it together. I didn't make a statement, though, that's not me. I wouldn't give the Bill anything. But if I'd seen him –

ELLIE: [*Interrupting*] Yeah, but Maureen, people are talking. They're saying you should've told them 'cause he was just a kid. I mean, that's not really grassing, is it?

MAUREEN: The guy was twenty-three years old, he had the mental age of a twelve year old, he was mentally retarded and paralysed down one side, so you're right; he was just like a kid. He only had £20 in his pocket and wanted to do business but Sadie took him upstairs and robbed him. I don't know what happened next but Dizzy said someone had beaten him up and robbed him. Then later, on the beat, he said it was Colin who did it. So I don't know what the fuck . . . The Monk is inside on remand and Sadie is out on bail. Her stuff is still with the forensics so until the results come back no-one really knows.

ELLIE: Yeah but it's a fuckin' horrible business though, isn't it?

MAUREEN: Just the fact that she robbed him is out of order. I can't stand that, it makes me sick. I never rob my punters; we've got a bad enough name as it is. Look at all that shit going on down the beat with them fuckin' vigilantes. They're trying to stop us from working when half of them are our punters anyway!

ELLIE: What's happened to that kid? Do you know?

MAUREEN: Well, he's got a broken neck, his collar-bone is broken, plus loads of other parts of him are all smashed up. They say he'll never walk again. He's in intensive care, like a fuckin' vegetable. The police told me he'd be better off dead. They said that whoever did it would've done him a favour. They're sure it was Dizzy. They *want* it to be him!

Giant

Saturday afternoon me and Ellie went over to Morrisons supermarket with this stolen cheque book and card to try and earn some money. It was one of those Switch cards, which meant that Morrisons was supposed to give us up to £50 in cash to do the shopping with, instead of us having to queue up at the bank first. I'd only just bought it off some guy before we set out, but then we got busted almost as soon as we walked into the fuckin' store. Well, I did. Ellie managed to get away.

I was feeling really good, you know, like I was invincible. But then the card showed up as stolen on the computer. The police arrived in flak jackets, those new American-style batons, handcuffs, and that was it . . . I was busted. They could've bailed me out that night but they wanted to know who my accomplice was. That's what the hold up was about: who was this mysterious woman? So Sunday morning, when he was having his breakfast, I had to speak to my solicitor to get me out of there. But then in the early hours of the morning I started to feel ill. I was down to my underpants and was sweating and sweating and I knew that my bowels were gonna start going soon so I asked to be put in a cell with a toilet, but they wouldn't let me.

I didn't wanna tell them about my habit but they'd already turned my gaff over and found my dope plants and a load of syringes, spoons and stuff. I said, 'Look, I've told you, I don't know any mysterious woman. You can do me for possession of the plants and attempted deception but I'm telling you now, I get those needles from the needle exchange scheme, from the Bradford Health Authority, so I think that covers me.'

I mean, that's right, isn't it? Why give out sets of works if it's illegal? But then they started taking liberties and asking me about heroin on the street and who's doing what. They were flicking through my address book, looking at this and that, and I swear I could see all those names flashing through my mind, 'Oh, I know this person . . . and that phone number.' They kept looking at each other, a nod here, a nod there. And I felt really crap, like I'd let the side down. I mean, fuckin' hell, they could've busted half of Bradford with the names in that book. I felt like a grass; I could see myself on Rule 43 and I hadn't even been charged yet.

In the event, they let me out at one o'clock Sunday morning. I wasn't expecting bail because I thought there were a lot of warrants out for me but apparently there'd been nothing on record since 1990, so I was free. The most amazing thing about all this was that when I got out I phoned up my drugs counsellor to apologise for standing her up the night before. We were supposed to go out for a meal but of course I couldn't

51

make it. She said, 'Never mind, I'll come and pick you up. We'll go have a meal, a drink and a smoke.' We've got the strangest relationship. She doesn't like me to talk about our friendship because she reckons it could compromise her position. But what the hell, who else has got a drugs counsellor like mine?

So, anyway, I got out but I was still withdrawing so I managed to beg 20ml of Methadone and rooted out some old filters and had a dig. I had a bath, then when I felt I'd picked up a bit, I got stoned on some really good bush. That sorted me out until about four o'clock in the morning. Then I was shitting myself and sweating like a pig. I had to get hold of Ellie and score a £20 bag of smack. We shared it. It was no big deal but at least it controlled my shitting. I had to throw away my best underpants behind some building site after!

Now I'm looking for another bag because all that one did was straighten me out and get my bodily functions in order. I need something to give me a buzz, if I could just get a bag now I know I'd get a tickle off it.

Lanre: The Glass Pipe

Spent a wild weekend in London town. It was a mixture of business and pleasure and a well deserved break from all that Bradford griminess. Dossed down with a couple of old friends, MoPic and his wife, though I didn't see much of her – she was out working most of the time. She's one of those churchy women who believes that if you're not hard at work then you must be hard at sin. So naturally I hung out with MoPic and kept my head down. I hadn't seen much of him either since I left Tottenham, which was at least three years ago. So it felt real good to be back on home turf again. Like somehow I'd arrived.

London town – home – had evolved into something like a jungle. In the first six months of that year more than 200 gun crimes had been reported, most of which were drug related and involved the young black gangsta youth – 'Yardies', as they liked to call themselves – both as perpetrators and victims.

Confusion reigned and the black community, struggling with conflicting emotions, failed to come to terms with the savage crack epidemic that was decimating its numbers.

I hadn't got into crack then. I'd tried it but only piddling experimental stuff to learn what all the fuss was about. It was no big thing really. But that weekend I was on one. I went so far so fast I nearly lost it altogether. And MoPic was no help either. He was so full-of-shit-scared I could smell it. I'd always known there was something about that guy, though I could never put my finger on it. It was like he was never completely with it, you know, like he was only half-way there, which made me wonder where the rest of him was at. Unfortunately that weekend I found out.

MoPic was a crack-head, he probably still is. To look at him you wouldn't have thought he was capable, but behind the scenes, with the curtains drawn and his back turned against the world, he was steeped in it. I didn't realise it at the time, on account of him hiding it so well. Even his wife didn't know about the problem and, as far as he was concerned, there was no problem, which was why she didn't need to know. What his wife didn't know therefore didn't exist. And if she was happy with that then that was fine by him too. As far as he was concerned piping was just something he did as a pastime, something to alleviate his boredom. But that 'pastime', such as it was, was an all day, every day, indulgence that was rapidly growing out of control. And there was absolutely nothing anyone could do to make him understand. He just didn't want to know. The pipe had become his only salvation.

We nicknamed him The Chancer, because he's the type of person who never asks before taking what he wants; the sort who'd chance anything to be sure of getting his own way. And, being ignorant to the real situation, we would laugh along with him, pretending he was only joking and that there was no malicious intention. We were unwittingly chancing our own lives too.

In London MoPic was all over me like a rash, like an epidemic about to explode. He could barely contain himself. Suddenly he pulled out a glass pipe, set it down in front of me, then sat there waiting. I had to laugh, I couldn't help myself. It was as if he'd chanced upon the plan of action that I hadn't even formulated yet and as usual didn't wait for an invitation. Eventually I did pull out some crack whilst he worked on the pipe: clean ash, filter, just the right amount of water. Then, after I chopped up the rock and loaded the pipe, he blasted off the first hit.

I'd never seen it done in a glass pipe before, much less tried it, so I was prepared to watch and learn.

MoPic pulled on that pipe as though his life depended on it, like it was his lover. He toyed with it, running the oil up and down, then up and down again, sucking and sucking, inhaling then sucking again, then held all that smoke there in his chest like he wasn't gonna give it up, like he *couldn't* give it up 'til he'd sucked it dry. Then, when his lungs were full, his chest burning and everything in there was fighting for space, he exhaled a great cloud of smoke and a 'Rastafari!' all in the same breath.

I was so impressed. I'd never seen anybody enjoy a pipe as much as that and couldn't wait to try it for myself. But he'd gone into one now. He stood with his face pressed up against the wall, his hands on his head, and eyes closed tight in meditation. It seemed like hours before he came back to me and realised that I was still there in the room with him, before I could wrestle the pipe from his grip. There was something different about him, in his eyes, like he'd been somewhere and gained some kind of secret knowledge. And, being impatient, I wanted to get some too, so I jumped straight in.

He did warn me about that, something about crack being a derivative of cocaine, which is an organic substance and takes years to grow. According to him, it should be smoked the same way, nice and easy. It sounded too long winded for me so I didn't take it in. I took a hit . . . and got nothing!

I didn't really know what I was looking for anyway, so I re-loaded the pipe and went for it again and again. We must've blazed at least £200 worth of that shit before I finally got it sussed; MoPic pacing me stone for stone all the way. Under the pretext of showing me how to smoke a glass pipe he got through my cocaine all by himself.

Right before my eyes I watched him burn rock after rock after rock. So I tried to keep up with him just to make sure I got a fair share.

But I must've been in too much of a hurry because suddenly I felt an almighty rush, which began in my groin and shot right through the top of head. I'd never felt anything like it before. It was frightening.

I'd been trying to copy MoPic, smoking the pipe just like he showed me. But whilst it was second nature for him, it was far too much for me. Holding my breath like that and cutting off the oxygen to my brain only exacerbated the situation. When I did finally get my breath back it was propelled by a crack-fuelled rush that exploded in my head like a rocket. My heart beat like crazy, like a tap dancer in my breast marking time: ONE . . . TWO . . . THREE . . . BANG . . . BANG . . . BANG . . .

My chest heaved and my breathing came in short, sharp, stabbing breaths; rasping breaths that made my whole body ache and the room spin. I began to panic and, for the first time that evening, I really thought of the possibility that I'd gone too far, that maybe I was not getting past this one.

I sat down and tried to get my head together but I couldn't settle, so I jumped up again. Then I lay down in the middle of the floor and tried to calm myself, willing my body to slow down and relax so I could regain some sort of control. But all that jiving around only made matters worse. I was in trouble and I knew it, but I didn't know what to do. So I prayed. I prayed to God and asked for His forgiveness; begged for one last chance. I pleaded with Him to touch me, just one touch, and make all this bullshit go away. I asked Him to save me and promised never to fuck up like this again. Never. I swore it. But then the palpitations started . . . ONE POTATO! I thought about my boys, my two secret weapons, and I swear I saw them swimming around my head like how Tom and Jerry see stars . . . TWO POTATO!

I thought how totally unimpressed they'd be if I were to die like this, if this was all their father had become. I thought about mother and the beatings she gave me as a child: 'Your head! Your head!' The welts erupting all over my body. Then the same again from my father. I begged Him for an opportunity to explain myself to them, and then tried to get my head around what was left of my life . . . PALPITATER! I looked over to where MoPic was standing, with the pipe still in his hand, and called his name. I was in a panic and wanted him to come and hold me. I wanted him to put his arm around me and comfort me because I didn't want to die alone, but he freaked.

He backed away from me, out of fear, and in his eyes I saw a panic even greater than my own. He had no idea what to do either and that really pissed me off because I realised that if I died there he'd most likely dump my body out in the street, rather than allow any connection back to him. MoPic may well have been a friend but obviously that friendship had its limitations and wasn't greater than the responsibility I had to my own life. That was down to me.

I was still pretty flaky when I finally stopped shaking and the palpitations began to subside. My heartbeat had slowed down, though, my breathing returned to normal, and there was no more panic. Perhaps it was that sudden rush of anger, or even God answering my prayers, but just as suddenly as it began that ghastly business was over. MoPic was still looking at me strangely but I didn't care about that now. I strode over to where he stood and snatched back what was left of my cocaine. I'd had enough. But something had changed.

Like MoPic, I felt as though I'd been somewhere and

gained some secret knowledge. I didn't know what it was exactly, or perhaps I just couldn't handle what I thought it might be, so, to be safe, I put it out of my mind, at least for the time being anyway.

It was more than I wanted to deal with.

Maureen

My friends were smoking crack cocaine like it was going out of style. They were on this massive rush but I refused to have anything to do with it. I wouldn't touch the stuff. I could see what it was doing to them, to their families, and I swore that I'd never let it get to me like that. For a whole year I watched them smoking. Sometimes they'd call round to my house with bags full of the stuff (God knows where they got the money from) and always the routine was the same. First of all they'd light up half-a-dozen cigarettes so they could collect the ash, then they'd set up their pipes and sit there smoking all night. In the morning, when the crack was finished, they'd club together and buy some more. Then, when that was done and they had no money left, they'd go home wired and on a downer because they were broke.

My boyfriend, Dave, was right into crack, really heavy on it, but he used to feel embarrassed doing it in front of me. He said I made him feel paranoid because I wouldn't smoke with him. If I ever went into the room where he was smoking he'd go ballistic, really freak out and get mad at me. So I had to wait until he was finished then try to make things right with him again. I used to get really annoyed. I'd ask him, 'What do you think you're doing? You don't need that stuff, why don't you throw it away? Just stop; it's easy!' Obviously I didn't understand it then, but I do now. I don't think I could throw it away either. It's not easy at all.

One day I thought I'd just have a go to see what the big attraction was. It was never meant to be a big thing, I was just curious. I wondered what everyone was making a fuss about. So I bought myself a stone, it was £25 in those days, put it all in a pipe and smoked it. Since that day things have never been the same. I just can't leave the stuff alone.

Lanre: Robbery

My working relationship with Spencer just wasn't working. In order to take the weight off my shoulders and inject some sort of new leadership, he introduced his younger brother to the business. But then, just as quickly, the whole thing collapsed altogether. I wasn't surprised. Strictly speaking I worked *for* Spencer and not with him, so that decision had nothing to do with me. I could've taken charge myself, since he was already spending most of his time away from the business and leaving it in my hands. I just couldn't cope with his complaining when things didn't go his way. I was also trying to work on my own agenda as well as working for him, so when he started playing an absentee boss I found it almost impossible to follow his lead.

Besides the fact that Spencer and I were complete opposites, with different ideas on what the business was about and how it should be conducted, we also weren't getting on very well. Superficially everything was fine, we even appeared to complement each other, but I knew the man from the inside. I knew he didn't have the balls, or the commitment to see the business through. So by the time it all fucked up I was already in a position to set up on my own.

Spencer and I were old friends, we went back a long way. We were old-time posse pals who misspent our youth together creating havoc on the streets of Bradford. We used to share the same house, made up of little one-room bedsits in those days, with four of us sharing the same room. We used to steal together, fight together, we even shared the same women. What was mine was his and what we didn't have we'd simply go out and get.

It didn't seem to matter that I was fighting a more personal battle than him and the rest of the posse, a battle fired up by the strict, unbending, rule of my parents, we just became a law unto ourselves.

We were just kids back then trying to make our mark in this world. But then I went to jail and by the time I got out the old crew had broken up and Spencer was a coke dealer.

We'd always known cocaine to be a playboy's drug for the rich and famous. It was never readily available to the likes of us second and third generation black youths. We couldn't afford the stuff so we never bothered ourselves with it. That is, until the mid-eighties when crack cocaine exploded on to the scene and suddenly we all wanted it. Surpassing all other drugs on the market, crack, rocks and stones, as we called it, emerged as the most popular drug in Bradford – and the most destructive. Crack became the drug of choice. If you had crack you had status.

I didn't know anything about crack, but I was interested. I wanted to know all there was to know about this drug that had captivated my friends, the people I knew and grew up with. So when I learnt that Spencer was peddling the stuff I went out of my way to ingratiate myself into his business. I became Spencer's gofer, his Joey, and worked a twenty-four-hour shift, never complained or argued, just simply did as I was told and learnt the mechanics as I went along. Every night, during a quiet spell, I'd indulge my secret plan by recalling that day's events, making notes to file away with any relevant details for future reference. So yeah, I suppose everything was cool while it lasted. But that was only the beginning.

In the meantime, little brother had taken charge of the business and at first I thought, well, okay, maybe it's not gonna be so bad after all. Maybe with him in the driving seat we can pool our resources and finally steer our business back on course.

But I soon discovered that he was just a smaller compact version of his older brother and knew absolutely nothing about the business of crack cocaine other than what he used for himself. So while little brother was floundering around trying to get to grips with his new business and yet still managing to dispatch a sizeable profit down to London, Spencer exiled himself to the bookies and made a big show of losing great wads of money on ever greater odds. Or he'd be at some crack party blazing away the product and trying to impress the shit out of everyone with his stature and weight; trying to command some kind of respect due to him being The Man. I didn't complain, what did it matter to me? My job was simply to sell as much crack as possible and stack up the money. So that's exactly what I did, all the while keeping my diary.

Eventually the business crashed and Spencer, having lost all sense of direction, pocketed what remained of the money and pissed off down to London. The coke was left in his brother's charge, with instructions to dispatch the lion's share of the profit down to him in London as it came in. And me, not wanting to be shackled to a brother who had nothing left to shout about, also gathered up what I could and split. So finally little brother was on his own, in charge of a business that barely existed, yet still busting his balls just to keep up the payments to his brother. I felt sorry for him in a way 'cause he really was so enthusiastic and just wanted to do the right thing. But that fuckin' Spencer had him trapped under his wing you know. And with only crack cocaine for company the little brother didn't stand a chance. In fact, we all became casualties.

Meanwhile, on the other side of town, some nasty little fucker was planning to seriously take me out of business. I'm driving a flash car, taking care of business, and instead of him saying something positive like, 'Yeah, one of the boys is making it – good for him,' that fuckin' low-life had got himself all twisted up and red-eyed with jealousy. His greatest desire was to see me take a fall, tumble all the way down to his level where, presumably, he wouldn't have to suffer the inconvenience of witnessing my new found success.

I had no idea what his problem was, why doing my own thing should cause him any distress. But if there really was any seriousness to his intent then I certainly was not gonna make the job any easier for him.

A punter told me that this wannabe was in with a couple of Yardies who were passing through town and was plotting to offer me up as bait, like a mackerel to the sharks. He said it was nothing personal, in that trite, insincere tone people use when they're relieved the pressure is on you and not them. 'It's just a money thing . . .' Yeah, right, as if I should be grateful for small mercies! But what surprised me most of all was that there was any punter out there even remotely interested in my welfare. It was difficult to believe this guy was on my side. What did he want, anyway?

I guess I had achieved a kind of notoriety within the Bradford drug scene but I'd never once entertained the notion that I was some kind of hero. In the greater scheme of things I was only a small-time dealer and still only a street hustler. So, as far as I was concerned, I had nothing to prove.

I wasn't into collecting enemies or their scalps, I was just there to learn. For me it was like hands-on research. But once again I reminded myself, as I shielded my eyes from his gaze, my hand masking my feelings, that I was the man getting fat on the money they hustled, or stole, to buy the drugs that kept me in business. While they risked life and liberty getting close to their buzz, then snuck off into some dark corner to enjoy their reward, I sat comfortable and secure in the knowledge that my next punter was just around the corner. They'd given up their freedom of choice, to do or not to do, and handed it over to me.

So whether I liked it or not I had to admit that I *was* 'the man' now and that title came with its own disadvantages.

I also sussed that if those Yardies really were planning to take me out then the problem wasn't only my own but also the wannabe's. If he didn't deliver the goods, so to speak, then he was in danger of getting burnt himself.

So, in a sense, he'd dug himself into the same hole that he'd prepared for me and created a sort of stalemate, with us both having it all to lose or nothing at all.

Pontificating the best and worst aspects of being on top of the pile may have been good for some but I held the opinion that it was all bullshit anyway and so carried on with my business as usual. Even when I learnt about the finer details of their plot I still wasn't too concerned. Every day some poor sucker was trying to pull something. We were living in hard times, where crack cocaine carried the swing and every fucker was trying to stamp out the next man. It was nothing new. So when those Yardies were ready to make their move I'd know about it.

But those guys were crazy. They didn't give a shit about anything or anyone except themselves. They carried hand guns, knives, machetes, and wouldn't think twice about using them. It was said they belonged to a gang of native-born Jamaicans, the TV and newspapers were full of their antics, about how they were killers, international robbers and should be left well alone. Those two in Bradford were like a couple of desperadoes running from city to city, looking for a soft spot to strike. They'd slip into a town where they weren't known, do a job on someone then move on before the victim sussed out what'd hit them. Or they'd get up close to someone who'd just made a raise and tax the fuckin' life out of them.

Back home in Jamaica they'd robbed the takings from the Reggae Sunsplash, then it was a big card game in Miami, a coke dealer in London, and so it went on, running, striking, running. No one complained. Even the police were defenceless or didn't care. By now they were running out of places to rest-up and hide, which is how they came to be here in Bradford, looking for a raise to open up the way for them.

I even spoke to them once when me and Greedy went to collect Mikey to start his shift. They came strolling out of the house next door to the wannabe's and looked like nothing at all, just a couple of raggedy kids in baggy jeans and training shoes, jostling each other and kicking stones along the street as they walked.

I couldn't believe that these were the two so-called murderers causing such havoc around the world, these two ragamuffins planning to turn me over!

Then one of them came over to the car and said he wanted to see me later. I asked if he was in the market for some crack and he replied, 'No man, this is a different business.' There was a tone in his voice. I looked him straight in the face and smiled to myself, as if I understood some part of a joke that he hadn't understood himself yet.

He didn't say anything else, he just stood there for a moment staring at me with this stone-faced expression.

Then he turned back towards his friend and the two of them, with their hands in their pockets, continued up the road, playing football with the stones along the pavement.

When Mikey came out of the house he had a crack pipe in his hand. I was still smarting from my previous encounter and didn't get into anything with him about his general slackness. I just tried to explain what had gone down, what we were up against and what might be expected of us. But he just wasn't with it.

He was stoned and dismissed the Yardies as boys. He wanted to jump straight in and kick arse – as if he was in any shape to go on with any shit like that. So Greedy took the pipe off him and nearly kicked his arse. Obviously the pressure was getting to us already.

We went back to work, picking up even more punters as the business progressed, but all the while keeping one eye on what was happening out there. We were waiting for a clue, the first sign that they were about to make their move. Greedy and Mikey had been with me for quite a while by now and had settled in nicely. The vibe was good, better than I had with Spencer and the attitude was one I knew I could depend on. So if anything was about to kick off we were ready and prepared. Greedy advised that I stay out of the way, just chill out in the background, but I insisted on being out there seeing people. And yet, at the same time, I didn't want to. I didn't know who to trust anymore. So, to cover ourselves and double-check all the angles, we decided to change the rota and instead of working shifts we worked as a team. All of us in one car at one time:

two up front and one in the back dealing with the punter. We played it strictly by our own rules and waited for something to happen. It didn't take long.

We were out on one of those long hauls taking half-an-ounce of unwashed cocaine to a punter in Skipton, about twenty miles north of Bradford.

Personally I didn't mind taking time out to make those sort of deliveries, even if there wasn't much profit in them. They didn't come too often, so for me they represented a break from the usual hustle and bustle; a gentle one-hour drive out of town, where I could be myself, shake off the pressures of the day and allow my mind to wander. It was what I called quality time. But Greedy and Co. weren't up for it. They saw it as an extravagance we couldn't afford, especially given the situation we had on hand. They preferred the punters to come to us, where we could keep a good eye on them without any risk to ourselves. In fact, Greedy reckoned we should cut out our Skipton punter completely. There was nothing in it for us anyway, so why bother? But *I* was in charge. So we drove out there, three-handed, a bit downcast at first but gradually getting into the spirit and the freshness of it. We had the music up, a couple of spliffs going, and we got as far as Bingley, just past the part-time police station, when the phone rang. It was the wannabe.

'Yo, Lanre,' his voice boomed, big and boastful, like this was the day I was gonna make him rich. I could imagine his chops gleaming.

'Lanre, can you do me a couple of ounces? I'm on a roll.'

'What?' pretending I had no idea what he was talking about.

'Two ounces of shit, of course, what d'you think?'

'No. I don't know. Why don't you try somewhere like Leeds?'

'Yeah? Well I was told you're the man for it, the only man.'

'Sorry, I can't help you.'

'Why, haven't you got it?'

'No. I told you.'

There was a short pause then he said, 'Okay, well do you want some?'

'What do you mean?' I asked him curiously.

'I know someone over in Leeds where you can get a good ounce from. He'll do you two for £2000, and it's good shit too.'

'Yeah? Well if you know where I can get one from why don't you get it for yourself?'

'Well, I just thought you might want one. I tell you what, I'll call you back in a couple of minutes and tell you where to meet me. We can get it straight away.'

'Are you sure? Is this straight up?'

'Yeah man, I wouldn't bullshit you, you know me!'

Fuckin' right I did. But still, 'Okay then, call me back in ten minutes.'

'Sweet. Ten minutes then, okay?'

He hung up.

So that's what it was all about, a pathetic two grand.

I was incensed by the pettiness of it all and obviously didn't bother to turn up for the meeting. In fact I continued with my business as usual, as though those dick-heads didn't exist, as though they posed no danger, no problem, and did my best to ignore their phone calls.

Once or twice, when they did get through, I set up meetings which I knew I would never keep. I was hoping that at some point they'd be smart enough to get the message and piss off somewhere else. But still they tried . . . They must've really needed the money.

The wannabe even threatened me once, suggesting that I owed him something on account of me disrespecting his phone call. I couldn't believe his nerve! If I'd seen him out on the street I would've broken his fuckin' head open. The little shit must've guessed that for himself, so he kept a sensible distance.

Gradually the phone calls stopped, the threats died down and I began to believe it was all over and done with. I really didn't want to get into any blood-battles with those guys, that wasn't what I was about. They could never have taken that money off me anyway so it would've been a lot of nonsense for nothing.

But after a few weeks news began to filter through that the Yardies had been busted. They were in a Welsh jail facing a number of charges including attempted murder. Apparently, after growing tired of waiting for me and listening to that air-head with his empty promises, they'd dragged him over to Wales to set up some other dealer to rob. The guy they targeted was a dealer in wholesale ganja. He'd put up a good fight but in the end they'd shot him. Nobody knew whether he was dead or alive, nobody knew what happened to the wannabe either. I never heard from him again.

Giant

So Fletcher says to Christine, 'Do you want him sorted out or what?' And without even thinking about it she says, 'Yeah.' But she don't really know what she's letting the poor bloke in for. Fletcher and Matty went round with these fuckin' great lumps of wood and you should've seen what a mess they made of him! Matty was swinging with this big piece of wood, like a fuckin' cricket bat, and he hit Fletcher on the leg. But Fletcher wasn't gonna lose face or nothing, so when he got back to the house he pulls his strides down and shows off this fuckin' great big bruise – and that was just the force of the blow on a backswing! What about the guy on the other end!

I went round later to see if he was alright. He was in a right fuckin' mess: broken legs, the lot. They were really worried, you know, they thought they'd killed him. But Colin didn't squeal, he didn't say a word. You don't squeal on them sort of people.

I remember Trevor Hutchinson (he's dead now, OD'd in Coventry). Look what they did to him! This is when Matty was on his feet, buying and selling gold. You know them ammunition boxes, the green ones with the clips on the end? Well, he had one of them filled with 'tom,' you know, gold, jewellery, Rolex watches, all quality stuff. And another one filled with dope, cannabis resin, pills, all sorts; he'd been buying up chemists' stashes just for fun. Matty was putting Trevor up, feeding him, turning him on, and he said that Trevor could help himself to the resin stashed in the box: 'And Trevor, if you want any Diconal, Palfium, or ought like that, just ask.' So Trevor was on to a really good thing. But he ended up pinching one of Matty's cheque books and cards. He'd also got a fistful of Diconal and all sorts of other goodies, and planned to fuck off, but he got pulled by the pigs on Kings Road. And Trevor, obviously not to be trusted, straightaway says, 'Oh yeah, I got them off Mathew Butters.' Grassed him up just like that. This was after Matty had been looking after him.

So, anyway, Trevor got himself bailed out and obviously had to keep out of the way, but Matty sent this guy called Alex over for him. Alex is dead now as well; he got beaten to death. I'm telling you, they're a fuckin' nasty bunch, these lot!

So Alex has no choice and is sent to collect Trevor. 'Go and get that fuckin' Trevor Hutchinson, we've heard he's in the Caribbean Club. Take him over to your house for a drink,' says Matty. Alex's girlfriend, Pam, a school teacher, is hiding under the bed completely freaked out. As soon as Fletcher and Matty got hold of Trevor they *really* went to town on him. They got a pair of scissors and even tried to cut his fuckin' ears off! Trevor shit himself, he had a fit of fear.

They tortured him and burnt him. They were trying to cut his lugs off but the scissors kept on folding over. Fletcher wanted to kill him: 'Let's finish the bastard off,' he said.

I'll never forget that. I just walked in on it, I couldn't believe it. 'You sit down, Giant,' they said. 'You ain't going nowhere while we get this sorted out.' But I just wanted to get the fuck out of there.

Pamela is hid under the bed and they're burning his fuckin' dick off!

They were pulling his foreskin back and shoving down lit cigarette ends and pulling the skin back over. He had a fuckin' fit. I've never seen nothing like it. It was awful, terrible. They took him up to the M606, naked, opened the car door and just kicked him out. The poor bloke was jabbering, he was a complete wreck. He was naked, his legs were all brown where he'd shit himself, his dick was burnt, his eyebrows were shaved, and Fletcher had tried to cut his ears off. But believe it or not the scissors had come off the worst.

I got collared for the Terry Fletcher Benevolent Fund yesterday. Can you believe it? Terry is Matty's brother-in-law and he wrote Matty a letter saying that he's back in jail and hasn't had a visit yet. He's got seventeen VO's, backdated 'cause they revoked his parole, and so far no-one's been to see him, so he's going mad in there.

He sent £50 out for Matty to get him some blow but that's just been spent. And Matty, who's worried sick about it, hasn't slept for five days and is in a right state. He's been robbing punters, beating people up, he even pawned his Rolex to try and get some of the money back for Terry. I said to him, 'Look Matty, you've been fuckin' spun mate, you've been tossed off.' But his manly pride won't have it. Him and Claire took this gold chain off a punter the other night. A big chunky chain that the punter thought he'd lost somewhere. Now Matty's admitted that Claire had it but he won't admit that she's spun him.

They've spent all that money Fletcher sent out on a couple of bags of skag so now they've got to make it back up again. Plus Matty's been hanging out with Claire. He sent her out on the beat this afternoon to get some money.

He's in a right fuckin' state . . . really ugly.

He was gonna punch my head in earlier on. He said, 'Don't talk to me like that.'

But I told him that I'll talk how I like. 'I've known you twenty-five years, you cunt. Why don't you fuckin' admit it, you've been spun . . . she's tossed you off.' They'd been saving up all this money to go and see Terry. It would've been one hell of a visit but when they got there somebody else was visiting him so they couldn't get in. So they came back with all this stuff and just did it in, you know, up their arms, on the foil, pipes, the fuckin' lot. I thought, 'Fuckin' hell, they're going again tomorrow and there'll be fuck all left for Terry.'

Claire's tossing him off alright. Doing punters, a few robberies here and there, then holding back the money. She'll go out and disappear for a few days then come back with fuck all – no gear, no money, nothing. He's admitted that much but he won't admit the rest. Fletcher's been ringing up the Burglars Arms every day from prison, shouting and bawling, 'Where's that fuckin' Matty?'

And that's why Matty's been hanging around Manningham all this time, he don't wanna answer the telephone.

Then Sicknote came up to me the other day and said that him and his mate were doing a bit of burglary and, if necessary, would I give them a hand?

Of course I said, 'Yeah, if it's beneficial to me, that is.' So they've done up some place at Thornton Road and found a safe but it's too heavy for them to carry. So Sicknote suggests they come down for me and, would you believe it, his mate says no, 'cause they'd have to split the money three ways! 'Fuck it,' he says, 'we can't afford another partner.' So they just left the safe sitting there. Rather than call me to help and split the loot they fuckin' left it. Now where's the intelligence in that? I mean, a third of something is better than nothing, isn't it?

But I'll tell you something about that fuckin' Sicknote.

It was through him I've learnt that smoking crack is a waste of time. When they did that burglary they got a computer, so I rang this guy and we sold it to him. We got the money and Sicknote suggests we buy a rock – this is 9.30 Saturday night. Eleven o'clock the next morning I'm still wandering around Manningham wired to fuck. But it was too early in the morning to call on anyone or do anything so I just sat down on a wall and I was thinking, 'Well, you've just spent £30 to feel fucked off like this.' And that's when it hit me – between 9.30 p.m. and 11 a.m. my share of the burglary had gone on rocks. I felt terrible and I'd spent *money* to feel like that! The only way to do crack is to fix up your arm with some skag.

But then I realised that it's no fuckin' good unless you have hundreds of pounds to spend on it.

Sadie

You see those dealers out there, they think they're it. They think they're so fucking clever, especially when you've got no money. You're nothing to them, just a crack-head, a junkie. They don't want to know. Well, I'll tell you something, they've got it all wrong. It's them who're the nobodies. I mean, who the fuck are they without us to buy their drugs off them in the first place? Where would they be then?

I spend all day, every day of the week up and down that fuckin' beat selling myself. I'm going with at least ten to fifteen strangers a day, putting up with fat, smelly bastards climbing over me, pawing me, wanting everything for nothing. The other day I had to fight this greasy Paki bastard off me because he wouldn't use a Durex. I got the money though, all £17.50 of it! I was so pissed off I went straight to buy myself a stone. I don't usually do that. I work all my punters first, my regulars, then I get my drugs and go home. But I was fucked up. I'd been out all night and got nothing. Not a bean. Then, when that silly cunt came along and didn't even have the right money, never mind refusing to use a condom, I just took what he had and split. I went up to the Front Line but there was no one there. I was so angry. Then I saw Mikey and his mate drive past but he wouldn't sell me anything because I didn't have the right money.

I couldn't believe it. After all the money I've spent with them. It's people like me who put those bastards up there in the first place and now they won't deal with me because I'm £2 short! They must think they're too good for me now. Another time they wouldn't deal with me because all my money was in coins. I mean, who do they think they are?

I was outside the Sunlight one night wondering who might still be switched on. I was rattling. Then Dizzy pulled up and invited me to go and have a smoke with him, so I jumped into his car and we went off to a hotel.

Everything was great at first, we were smoking and chilling, but then suddenly he started grabbing me, you know, and I wasn't into that. I just wanted a smoke. He kept on trying to get next to me and all that, so I gave him a kiss. It was nothing special, just a peck on the cheek. The next thing I know he starts coming out with all these demands and said that if I didn't do what he wanted then he'd make me pay for all the coke I'd smoked. Well, I only had £17 on me so I gave him that and got up to leave, but the bastard had locked the door so I couldn't get out. He just sat there laughing at me and smoking his pipe. I mean, what could I do?

I sat down next to him and said we could do it if he didn't force me. I'd been fuckin' punters all night and wasn't in the mood for any rough stuff from him but it seemed to me that was the only way I was going to get out of there. I took my jacket off again and had a smoke with him, then he grabbed me and started pulling off my clothes. I was really scared. I fought like mad but he had me pinned down and was trying to pull my skirt off. I was wearing a belt with my skirt so it was pretty difficult for him to get it off, plus I was struggling. I asked him not to hurt me and said, 'If you stop I'll take my skirt off myself. Just don't hurt me.' So then he got off and stood by the window and I had to take my clothes off. There was nothing else I could do. I took my clothes off and sat on the bed with him. Then we had another pipe and we just did it. He was so rough he hurt me inside. He didn't even take his own clothes off. He just made me do all these things to him while he smoked his pipe. Then when he finished he kicked me out.

About a week later I was at my boyfriend's house. I didn't tell him what'd happened because I didn't want to cause any trouble. He would've said it was my own fault, anyway. I'd just got out of the bath after finishing work that night and was getting ready for bed when someone rang the door bell. Jav, my boyfriend, looked out of the window and said it was Dizzy. I just froze. I wanted to tell Jav not to answer the door, but because I hadn't told him what had happened I couldn't say anything.

Dizzy came upstairs, right into the bedroom, and told me to get dressed, I was to go with him. I didn't know what he was on about, I thought he'd gone mad or something, but he was serious. Jav stepped in and asked him what he thought he was playing at and got punched in his mouth for it. I was shitting myself and asked him why was he doing this? He said I owed him money for those rocks I'd smoked in the hotel room with him that night, and that I had to go back out on to the beat to earn the money back for him. He said I owed him £200 but he would accept £100, half of it.

Well, to cut a long story short, I didn't even bother arguing with him. We both knew I didn't owe him anything but with Jav getting beaten up like that and not being able to help me, I just went to my bag and got the money for him. I gave him exactly £100. But he'd followed me into the room and when he saw how much money I had he just took the lot. I'd made about £120 that night plus the heroin and crack I'd already scored. He didn't get any of that, he just took the money and left. Then me and Jav had this blazing row so I went and stayed with my friend Maureen. When I told her what had happened she said that Dizzy had done the exact same thing to her: he'd invited her for a smoke, took her to a hotel room and raped her. He called at her house every day for a month after that and took all her money off her. In the end she had to go to the police and have him arrested. That's what they're like, but I tell you what, if that Dizzy bastard ever comes near me again I'll put him in jail myself. I don't care. They're bastards, all of them!

Lanre: Car Crash

It was a simple car crash, nothing special. Obviously the cab driver knew it was illegal to do a U-turn on the wrong side of the road but he tried it anyway and caused me to crash into the side of him. There was nothing I could do, the idiot was right there in front of me. I applied the brakes, made a big skid, then . . . CRASH. Directly opposite the Law Croft Police Station! In addition to the half-an-ounce of heroin and cocaine I had stashed down my pants, the car had no tax, no MOT, and I had no driver's licence. So I guess I shouldn't have been on the road in the first place. But still, whose business is that anyway?

The cab driver, a fat Asian guy, leapt out of his car to survey the damage just as I was trying to unravel myself out of mine and make a run for it. I had to get away from there but I couldn't move. The impact of the crash had jammed my foot down between the accelerator and the brake pedal. I was hanging both in and out of the car with my face grazing the road surface and watching him mutate into an even bigger monster as his anger rose. The thought of that bastard sitting on me until the police arrived was too much. I was trapped right outside their front door, all they had to do was stretch out that long arm and haul me in.

The car was a write-off. I felt really bad about that because I'd only just borrowed it from my neighbour and was expected to return it that evening. But I couldn't worry about that now, I still had the cab driver to deal with.

It was important that I got in there first and took charge of the situation; grandstand him with a big act, even use my injuries if necessary. So I started screaming at him about his driving, about how he'd nearly killed me and mashed up my ankle. His apologies didn't work. He looked for something else to say but I was all over him, he didn't stand a chance. In desperation he threw his arms up in the air and said he was going to call the police. That was the very last thing I wanted so I changed tactics and tried to bluff it out, but he wasn't having it. Suddenly he dived back inside his taxi and, in his own language, started speaking real fast into the radio. He was yelling and pointing like he was trying to describe me to someone on the other end.

I was more concerned about the attention we were attracting and began to worry about the police being right next door. So far I was okay, only a passing couple had stopped to watch the show, but still I wanted to get away from there, fast. The cab driver was still busy with the radio, he'd turned his back on me and appeared to be taking down some instructions. So I seized that opportunity and ran.

All hell seemed to break loose behind me as I ran, limped, hobbled, anything I could manage to put some distance between me and him. But with my leg as it was I could only manage a few yards so I had no choice but to use both feet and run, sprained ankle or no sprained ankle.

I ran until I couldn't feel the pain in my leg any more, until I was clear of any sound behind me, and I felt that me and my drugs were safe.

About a mile away from the scene, somewhere in the vicinity of the Royal Infirmary, I remembered the Monk used to hang out around here. Wasn't he dossing with a couple of friends nearby, or was it just one of those move in, rip you off, move out situations?

I thought if I could just find the house I'd be able to phone for a taxi home. But then it dawned on me, maybe that bastard cab driver had distressed his cabbie friends and now they were all on the look out for me. Perhaps that's what he was doing on his radio, and inciting the police to join the hunt too.

It was ridiculous, I know, but that's how it was when the paranoia began. Like I was the perpetrator of a crime so dramatic that the whole of Bradford city was hunting me down. Up ahead in the distance I heard the blast of a siren and thought the cops were already bearing down on me, so I took off again, running. I almost tripped over another one patrolling his beat. I immediately stopped running and crossed over the road. Just like my mother taught us when we were young, 'If you see a policeman in the street, cross over, then you can't be blamed for anything.' I could hear her voice ringing in my head, as I always did whenever I was in trouble. Ironically, her insistence that her children should run away from the law, even when they were innocent, must've been some sort of precursor to the guilt I'd feel as an adult. And right there the irony played itself out: I was running away from a policeman who didn't know that I was guilty of anything. It was as stupid as that.

I'd strayed so far away from where I thought my friend's house was I decided to sack that idea and take the bus home instead. My foot hurt like hell, it took all my effort to walk on it now, but I was still carrying that minimum five years prison sentence in my crotch so I had no choice. The quicker I got that safely home the better.

I took a chance and headed back towards the city centre. I knew that taking a bus was a much better decision than hopping around in circles hoping for a miracle.

And I was in luck, too. Just as I came upon the first stop a bus came swinging around the corner. I had no idea where it was going. I didn't even recognise its number. But it was transport out of that danger zone, so I stuck my hand out for it. Finally I was on my way home. Thank you Jesus . . . Thank you.

Lance

Me and Ellie are always getting hassle from the Asian dealers. It doesn't seem to matter that we're regular punters, that we score from them every day. They just take our money then give us a hard time.

I remember once I had a load of aggro off Zaff. He'd heard that story about me losing £40 in the back of his mates' car. So he came over and said, 'They're telling everyone that you're a right silly cunt 'cause they've got your money. So I went and sorted them out. I told them they are a bunch of bastards. I've done you that favour so from now on you score your gear from me, right?'

I told him to fuck off. Who does he think he is? I'll score from whoever I want to score from. I knew he was talking bollocks 'cause if those guys had said that about me then you can rest assured he was in there with them. There's no way a Paki will defend a white man against another Paki. Not in this lifetime anyway.

Ellie

It seems to me the police are trying extra hard to find some means of getting me on a supplying charge, but at the end of the day they only do me for possession.

The day they decided to raid me I was in the kitchen preparing a dig. Suddenly the front door burst open and about eight police stormed in. 'Police! Police!' they screamed. 'Stay where you are!' Well, I had my works and stuff out on the kitchen table so that was the last thing I was gonna do. And fortunately for me they'd only broken through the front door and still had to get down the hallway so that gave me some time to cover my tracks. Lance was in the front-room freaking out and didn't have time to respond. He just shouted the same thing as the police, 'Ellie, it's the police!' before they got to him and made him stand still with his hands where they could see them. I was still in the kitchen, they hadn't seen me yet.

Lanre: Drugs Bust

The first thing the cops wanted to know when they burst into my house was where I'd hidden the charlie. There were six of them, four guys and two women; the women taking turns to play at good-cop/bad-cop and the guys being regular officers. It was a classic set up, something like a synchronised swimming team and almost as boring.

'I don't know what you're talking about,' I said with my arms outstretched, innocent like. 'I live here, not Charlie.' They laughed at that one, they thought it was funny. But the boss, let's call him 'Smith' (but that's not his real name), was not amused. Tall, thin, cropped grey hair, very pallid, he worked extra hard to distinguish himself from the others; to assert the fact that he was in charge and everything was under his control. He kept laying that on me over and over again just in case I misunderstood him the first time, like it was seriously important that I should know. I guess he wanted to show just how hip he was, that he was truly down with the scene and knew that I had ounces of the stuff stashed somewhere around the house.

He asked me again: 'Where's the charlie?'

This time laying emphasis on the cocaine angle. He was talking drugs.

'What?' He said he wanted to give me the opportunity of coming clean before he gave orders to begin the search. I played it cool. I didn't lose my head or anything, just answered that he and his gang of burglars had arrived with the intention of searching my house anyway, so they may as well get on with it. 'And I still don't know what the fuck you're talking about. You won't find any drugs in this house!'

Then, to show my indignation, I sat down and made myself comfortable. I guessed I was gonna be in for a long afternoon.

I don't think he liked that very much, it kind of undermined his authority. The other cops were smirking behind his back, anyway. I should've been trembling, I suppose, scared shitless that any minute now he was gonna find me out and I'd be for the hole. Instead I thought it was quite funny. My non-reaction to his illustrious self must've gone completely against everything they'd taught him at detective school. It was hilarious.

While his men were rummaging through the room and turning things over, he'd be standing to one side, or in a corner, just staring at me, trying to figure out the look on my face, trying to read my thoughts. And if I blinked or rubbed my eyes in any particular way he'd suddenly leap on to something in my line of vision, pick it up, then scrutinize my face again. Of course I'd simply look somewhere else, blink, rub my eyes, and he'd be off again, leaping, inspecting and scrutinizing, until he got bored and changed tactics.

Then he squatted down directly in front of me, almost nose to nose, eyeball to eyeball, drilling a hole through my skull and trying to unfold my brain. I couldn't see what the others were up to with him in my face like that, so I shifted my weight to my left-hand side and peered around him. And that damn-fool-cop, interpreting my movements as shifty, dived on to whatever it was he thought I was trying *not* to look at.

He really was convinced I had cocaine in the house and thought he had me sussed. Every now and again he'd pick up a shoe box or a container of something, rattle it, then ask me what it contained before checking it out for himself. He was so ridiculous I just couldn't be bothered with any more of his questions, they were so fuckin' mechanical and textbook like. So I ignored him and focused my attention on the she-cop searching beneath the sofa. She was young and pretty, a slim athletic type, and had to reach far beneath the cushions to do the job right. So I've got my eyes glued to her thighs waiting for a revelation of stocking tops and perhaps an inch or so of panties.

At least that was a better prospect than the dickhead in the corner leaping around like an idiot in distress, trying to psyche me out.

I wondered to myself, why do ambitious young women like her waste themselves in the police force? I mean, she must've really believed in the job once, thought that her contribution would make a difference.

I was interested and wanted to find out more, but before I could put the question to her the front door flew open and Yasmin waltzed in. She was halfway through an apology for being late then froze mid-sentence when she realised the scene she'd just walked into. Then she began to cry. I should've known better. I should never have allowed myself to be taken in by those tears, but I did. And like a fool I even tried to cover up for her, claiming that she had nothing to do with anything and had only called round to see my girlfriend.

Then suddenly it was like 'Go! Go! Go!' Two cops jumped on her like they were S.A.S. and frog-marched her upstairs. At that moment another one of them came out of the kitchen holding up a plastic container of fluffy white powder and 'Smith', with his eyes gleaming, moved in on me, but then discovered it was only Yam Flower – Nigerian soul food! After a while Yasmin was dragged downstairs again, minus her Vodaphone, and with her clothes all disarrayed, and was taken off to the police station.

Something was wrong! I didn't know exactly and there was nothing much I could do about it anyway, but I knew there was *something* wrong. Then, as if on cue, the other she-cop came down from the bathroom with a big grin on her face, brandishing £1200 cash in one hand, and a bag of prime sensimillia in the other. 'Smith' was ecstatic and almost orgasmed right there in front of us all.

Okay, so he hadn't discovered any cocaine but he had got a bag of excellent ganja, and as far as he was concerned a bust was a bust.

Conversation

Giant's apartment, in the late afternoon

Giant and Lance, quick-stepping through a busy, noisy Front Line, finally reach Giant's apartment without once being challenged to buy more drugs. In one hand Giant carries a Netto bag of groceries and, in the other, jammed deep in his pocket, a quarter-gram of smack to share with his friend. Giant puts the shopping down in the kitchen then begins to prepare a dig for himself. What's left of the smack he hands to Lance, who intends to smoke his on a foil, 'chasing the dragon' style, for a change.

GIANT: [*Calling from the kitchen*] So I says to Monk, this is a fuckin' wind up!

LANCE: [*Preparing kitchen foil for his smoke*] You're blazing rocks, and what . . . you feel like you're being ripped off?

GIANT: Well, I wanted a turn on. I mean, Dave had just scored himself a £50 rock and they got a pipe together round at Monk's. I bumped into them there and was the only one who had a decent lighter. So I'm lighting these fuckin' pipes and I says, 'Is there anything for me?' you know? Monk starts sulking and tells *me* not to sulk. So I says, 'I am fuckin' sulking!'

LANCE: So why can't you have a pipe then?

GIANT: [*Concentrating on his dig*] He just . . . wound me up . . . tremendously! There I am, burning their rock for them, and making sure Dave don't burn his hair as well, and they're not offering me fuck all! I says, 'Just a minute, where's mine? You come in here with a nice chunk of rock, I even build a pipe for you, and you don't wanna give me nothing . . .'. Of course I was fuckin' sulking! So, in the end, he gets a pipe together for me then he goes out and buys another lump of rock. So we was smoking loads of pipes last night but, you know, in the end I didn't even enjoy it. Just the same as I don't enjoy listening to you and Ellie arguing about smack . . .

Suddenly Giant falls into a nod. Still wearing the tourniquet and with the needle sticking out of his arm, Giant is in a world of his own and no longer part of the conversation.

LANCE: Yeah, yeah, I know. But arguments are necessary sometimes, they help clear the air. Just that our arguments are a waste of time, 'cause half of it is always denied. You'd think I was arguing with myself. She always turns what I say upside down and throws it back at me, like I'm telling lies or something. I feel like she's taking me for an idiot. She must be pretty daft herself if she really thinks that I'm fuckin' stupid enough to fall for half the shit she comes out with.

Obviously we must have a problem, Giant, otherwise I wouldn't be going on like this, would I? You hit the nail right on the head. I know we're incompatible, I've known it for a long time. It takes a lot more than her fucked up past to make things work for me. But I don't believe for one minute that she can make a relationship without heroin. And even if she can, what the fuck kind of relationship is that gonna be? I'm sure she doesn't even know herself. She's never tried it before. You've even said it yourself, Giant, 'When you go back down South, where does Ellie fit in?'

Realising that he's been talking to himself, Lance turns round and finds Giant sliding down off the chair, half sprawled-out on the floor.

Jesus Christ, are you alright, Giant?

GIANT: [*Angry that his buzz has been interrupted*] Yeah, 'course I am! I'm just on a gouch, that's all. I wish you'd leave me alone!

LANCE: Leave you alone? Listen man, I don't want any of that nonsense around me. Look at the fuckin' state of you!

GIANT: I keep telling you I'm alright. I'm not going over. I'm just enjoying the buzz.

Lance finally gets hold of his half of the heroin, puts it on the foil and starts to smoke. Ignoring Giant's gouch, and near overdose, he returns to his seat and carries on with their conversation, as though there were no interruptions.

LANCE: Yeah, well I guess we have been arguing a lot recently but I'm not gonna be taken for an arsehole, it offends my integrity. It's as simple as that. I don't give a fuck about all the rest of it, who's cheating who, whether she's a lying bitch or not. Who gives a fuck? I will not be undermined like that. Who the fuck does she think I am?

If all this arguing is about heroin, as you keep on saying, then it's up to me to do something about it. The truth is that every day I say I'm giving up this shit, every day I resolve to have nothing more to do with it, then someone turns up with a wrap and I'm back in it again. It's not easy. The only way that I'll really get off this shit is to go off by myself, because I don't feel that I've got anything here, or that what I've got here isn't compatible with what I really want . . . It's got everything to do with smack, if you take that shit away from this relationship then there isn't very much left, is there?

Giant gouches out again while Lance contemplates his situation. After a while the heroin gets the better of Lance and he too gouches out. Now there is only silence.

Giant

David comes down to my gaff for a couple of wraps and decides that he wants to do one straight away. Now this guy has only got one arm, the other one's a stump and is no use to him at all, but he's got cranking down to a fine art – the man's bordering on perfection. Anyway, he gets the smack together in a spoon and I say, 'Do you want a hand with that?'

But he wants to be independent and says, 'No, I'm okay, I can do it myself.'

For some funny reason I thought he'd use his good hand to dig it into his stump because he still has some good veins floating around in there, you know what I mean?

I wasn't stood there gawping at him or anything, I just thought, 'How the fuck is he gonna manage that?' With all his equipment laid out on the table, he sucked up the smack from the spoon into a set of works, one-handed – he's even got that mastered! Then he just totally amazed me. He's got the works, loaded up with a needle and everything in his mouth, and he's stuck it straight into a vein in his stump with total precision.

Whatever technique he's developed, whether he's

using his lips or his tongue, he's drawn his blood into the works, then he's used his tongue to push the plunger in, flushed it a couple of times, pulls the works back out again with his teeth, and spits it out on to the side of the table . . . then he asked me for a cigarette! It was fuckin' amazing . . . I'd never seen anything like it in my life before! It was so perfect it only took him about thirty seconds.

Look at me, I've got two healthy hands and it always takes me ages to get it right. I seem to get blood all over the fuckin' place. I mean, it's got to the stage now where I've thrown the set of works into a corner of the bloody kitchen 'cause it's all congealed, or I can't find a vein, you know.

But David, with his one arm and a stump, he's perfection itself. There's no such thing as congealed, can't find a vein, or anything like that. What amazes me about him is that he's been using gear for years, then eleven years ago he lost his arm in an accident and realised that he couldn't have a dig. I know anybody can do anything with perseverance and training and no doubt he's had his girlfriend doing it for him and all the rest of it, but he's had to develop a technique for himself and master it too.

Lanre: Sonny's Gun

I'd been running around all week trying to get my shit together and finally everything was set. Then, on the day, there was so sign of Sonny; four, five hours later, still no sign. I knew I was in trouble but I hung in there anyway. What else could I do? I'd tried everything; phoned everyone I knew that knew him. His wife said to try his mobile, as if I hadn't thought of that already. Still, I tried again and, as expected, got nothing: 'The Vodaphone you're calling may be switched off. Please try again later.' FUCK IT!

All that waiting was a bitch and I just couldn't take any more. All the time wondering, has he been busted? Will he talk? Will they come for me? That's how the hustler pays his dues; when he knows he's gonna get burnt but he doesn't know how or when, or by whom. When he knows it's his *arse* on the line.

At about 5 p.m. the phone rang and I almost leapt out of my skin trying to reach the damn thing before it stopped. 'What the fuck's happening?' It was Spencer, sounding vexed.

I tried to explain the delay but he cut in, threatening that if I didn't get it together I'd be in deep shit. His people were not impressed with my dilly-dallying. If I screwed up then he wouldn't take the rap for me, I'd be on my own. There wasn't much I could say to that, the truth was worse than how I felt, so I said nothing.

Then a car pulled up outside, Sonny walked in, and I screamed down the phone, 'Sit tight man, I'm on my way! I'm on my way!'

First thing that morning I'd put an order through to Spencer for a quarter-kilo of cocaine. He promised to take care of it and guaranteed the shit would be waiting for me, as long as I could guarantee my own end. There were to be no fuck ups.

So naturally I said nothing about how Sonny had almost done just that. I stood on the accelerator and drove like the wind, praying that everything would work out now.

We made that 200 mile journey from Bradford to West London in two hours flat, yet still we were too late to catch Spencer at home.

I was well pissed off at that.

He must've known that it was normally a three hour drive; surely he could've made allowances. Anyway, I refused to be stuck with Sonny overnight, I'd had just about all I could take, so I dropped him off at his relative's house then drove over to Brixton and spent the night there with a girlfriend. The following morning, completely refreshed, I picked up MoPic, rather than Sonny, and set off determined to get the business sorted.

But at 2 p.m. that afternoon we were still sitting there

in Spencer's front room, like fuckin' lemons, waiting for something to happen. After all that bollocks I'd gone through just to get there, those bastards couldn't even get to the starting line! Spencer did his best to look like he was on top of the situation. Like his firm hadn't let us down really, and that maybe we were still in with a chance. But I was too fuckin' angry to concern myself with reassurances. I needed action. I was thinking about the money and my profit margin.

I had Sonny's £5,000 for his four ounces in my pocket and I'd picked up another £4,800 from two other punters for a couple of ounces each. I was buying the cocaine at weight, as opposed to nine individual ounces, a saving of £800, plus I was into an ounce for myself. Altogether I was making a tidy little sum. So yeah, I didn't *mind* playing like lemons whilst we waited but I desperately needed to get things moving. I caught Spencer slipping out the front door to use the call box on the corner instead of his mobile and I just hoped to God that it was our business he was dealing with and not some other bullshit that would leave us sitting there waiting.

Sonny was not impressed with me leaving him behind and demanded to know where I was. He thought I was trying to skank him and refused to wait any more; he wanted to be there. *He* wouldn't wait!

What the fuck had I been doing for the past two days?

Then he wanted a blow-by-blow account of what was happening with his money.

He'd been trying to get hold of me all morning, the

last attempt being a demand for his money back. Well fuck him, I was sorting myself first!

Spencer finally got through to someone who did have the amounts we wanted and I immediately began to worry about my profit margin again, although I needn't have bothered. That joker wanted me to pay for the sample I insisted on testing. When he realised that wasn't gonna happen he packed up and left. Not to worry. That's how they are, these 'I wannabe-a-dealer' types. They've only been in the business two minutes, got themselves a wad of money, and suddenly they wanna call the shots. If that chancer had any sense he would've been ten grand richer! I didn't bother to report that back to Sonny but he phoned me anyway, about an hour later, asking what the hold up was. I just switched off the phone. The less nonsense I heard from him the better.

Time was moving on but at 7 p.m. we were still absolutely nowhere. But then, as so often happens in apparently hopeless situations like that, things suddenly took a dramatic turn and everything began to fall into place. I don't remember the exact sequence of events, just that Spencer got this phone call from some woman who had a load of washed-rock and, if we were interested, we had to meet her in a pub somewhere near the Oval. Naturally I agreed, since there was nothing else doing. So then we were winging through South London. I thought I'd better switch my phone on to stay in contact with her. The damn thing had only been on five minutes when it started screaming at me and I just knew it had to be Sonny. For a while back there the silence had been almost ecstatic. But now he took the liberty of getting inside my head again and nearly blowing our lead.

His mouth ran riot, the threats coming thick and fast, staccato style:

'WHERE THE FUCK HAVE YOU BEEN? WHAT'S GOING ON? WHERE'S MY MONEY? DID YOU GET THE SHIT? WHERE THE FUCKIN' HELL ARE YOU, ANYWAY? LISTEN, I'M GOING BACK TO BRADFORD SO I NEED MY MONEY, OKAY? OKAY? WHO-THE-FUCKIN'-HELL-DO-YOU-THINK-YOU-ARE, ANYWAY!? DON'T FUCK WITH ME, MAN, YOU UNDERSTAND? DON'T FUCK WITH ME!'

That bastard had me so worked up my hearing shot through and everything in front of my eyes turned the brightest red. And still he babbled on and on. I took a deep breath, I took ten deep breaths, and started a one . . . two . . . three . . . count. Then I pretended there was some kind of interference on the line: 'What . . .? I can't hear you . . . speak up . . . I can't hear a word you're saying . . .' and hung up.

The last thing I heard him screaming at me was to meet him outside Kings Cross Train Station in twenty minutes. Well, hardy fuckin' ha, ha. We were miles away and heading in the opposite direction. Besides, I wasn't gonna meet him, or take his money out of the equation, because that would've really screwed things up. So I passed the phone over to MoPic and instructed that any time Sonny rang, which was pretty rapid now, he should tell him I was busy and that I'd get back to him later.

We double-parked outside the pub. One of those

wine-bar-cum-night-club spots, with neon signs and lights flashing everywhere. The place was jumping, trendy young things spilling out on to the pavement, drinks, spliffs, and anything else at hand.

I didn't like it – it was too busy for me – but Spencer ducked inside and came out a few minutes later with two Ragamuffin kids and this skinny dark-skinned girl who looked no more than school age. I just didn't like it; I didn't like it one bit. What the hell could this trio of kids do for me?

I thought maybe it was some kind of set up, with her as bait. I stepped back against the wall so I could study them more closely when suddenly she whipped out a tightly wrapped parcel from under her skirt and began offering us all a free sample, like it was Christmas already. I was amazed . . . the shit was top class. But she only had like fifty grams altogether, so I bought the whole parcel from her.

I wasn't sure how I was gonna explain it all to Sonny, or to those two waiting up there in Yorkshire, but at least I'd got something and could now think about heading home . . . But first I had to deal with Sonny.

I dropped Spencer off at home then drove over to Kings Cross to see if we could find him. I had no idea what to expect.

I knew he was angry but you never can tell – it could've been a bluff. In this business you learn everything there is to learn about bluff and attitude, you get to learn it instinctively. The more determined punters will often work something out with a dealer and end up with drugs of their own to sell. Then, through the madness of their buzz, they start having these macho visions of themselves. Sonny was like that sometimes, that's where the danger lay, the taxing and the maiming.

At one o'clock in the morning we pulled into Kings Cross, opposite the burger bar, as arranged, and waited for Sonny to show himself. After a while I phoned his mobile but he was switched off. So I guessed he was already in the station somewhere looking for me.

Maybe it wasn't such a good idea to have kept him waiting like that.

Unusually for that time of night the station forecourt was quiet except for a couple of down-and-outs and an old prostitute squabbling over floor space immediately behind the rubbish bins. I specifically remember that incident because it was so funny.

Watching those three fighting over a tiny piece of turf like that made me realise just how pathetic and futile the crack business really is. Up until that moment I hadn't realised just how exhausting the past thirty-two hours had been. That scene at the station's entrance provided us both with all the entertainment we needed to let go of the tension and relax. And as the stress began to fall away I felt a *déjà vu* . . . like I'd waited for Sonny before.

I got out of the car to stretch my legs and told MoPic to take my place at the wheel.

'If Sonny arrives whilst I'm gone get him into the passenger seat next to you and sit tight. I won't be long.' I was working on instinct and needed Sonny up-front where I could see him. If he had any tricks up his sleeve then I wanted the advantage on my side.

I'd only just got back to the car, with burgers and milk shakes, and was settling down in the back when there was an almighty crash against the side window. Sonny's distorted face loomed up large against the glass.

I freaked and wondered what the fuck it was, that grotesque thing staring at me like some dark demon of the night. When I realised it was Sonny I relaxed, leaned over, and opened the passenger door for him, but he just stood there staring at me. Then, real slow and menacing like, he climbed in.

The man looked wild, like he'd completely lost it.

He just sat there staring at me, pinning me to the seat with those eyes of his, and this voodoo expression. I couldn't fathom it.

I looked to MoPic for a clue but he sat staring at his hamburger, as though somehow he'd only just realised it was there.

I turned back to Sonny and just about caught the faintest narrowing of his eyes before his hand came up from behind the car seat with a gun pointing at my face.

I froze. My head still at an angle. Caught mid-turn. Trying to catch my breath. I couldn't believe it. Was he serious? Was he really gonna take me out or what? My mind flashed through that day's events, through the past thirty-two hours, searching every act, every word, trying to find out why my arse was hanging in the balance like that. And there the frame froze and I sat waiting for the curtains to fall.

I guess normally in a situation like that I would've been scared shitless and ready to bail out at the first opportunity. It's not every day some wild man pulls out a gun in the middle of the street and threatens to shoot you stone dead. Even MoPic, pretending to be somewhere else, jumped so high out of his seat he almost went through the sun-roof. But I just wasn't buying into any of that bullshit – I knew Sonny.

He was a guy who only dreamt of being a drug dealer. He wanted to be the Man, the top dog, at the head of the pack where he'd be feared and respected. That was his vision, his recurring day-dream. In reality he was a crack-head. A fully fledged rock junkie whose habit had led him so far up his own arse he'd lost all touch with reality. Somewhere inside himself he knew this to be true. For one brief moment I thought that was it, the end, that I was finished. But I promised to remember his gun-toting wet dream and one day drown him in it. If he ever got a hard-on for me like that again I'd tie the fuckin' thing around his neck.

I heard a voice from somewhere, my own voice, say, 'Fuck this, man, let's have a smoke and try to work this one out.' He didn't answer. He just continued looking at me for a long moment, pointing that gun at me. But I swear I saw a flicker of hesitation in his eyes, just a brief thing, then it was gone. Like maybe he wasn't quite so sure anymore. Then, as if to underline his uncertainty, he whispered, 'Have you got my money?' In that instant I realised he really did believe I'd ripped him off; that he never expected to see his £5000 again or any of the cocaine. I kind of felt sorry for him in a way. How could he be so dumb? How could he really believe I'd disappear with his money? Why did he give it to me in the first place?

And if I had intended to skank him wouldn't I have been long gone by now instead of sitting there, in the back seat of my own car, with his fuckin' gun in my face? The idea was so stupid I nearly lost my head laughing. Then off the top of my head I said, 'I bet the gun isn't even loaded!' And then it hit me . . . 'I BET IT ISN'T EVEN A REAL GUN!' What a fuckin' idiot! I felt like a real fool! Maybe it was a toy, or one of those cigarette lighters masquerading as a gun, something he bought from some Mickey Mouse joke shop. I looked at it again, I couldn't see all of it, only the barrel, snub-nosed and pretty mean looking, wavering just six inches away from my nose. I kept noticing how he kept most of it hidden up his sleeve with only the end of the barrel showing. Its surface was all scratched up, with small strips peeling off and showing a different colour underneath.

And then I sussed the diameter of the barrel was too big for ordinary bullets to pass through . . . unless he planned to shoot me with cannon balls!

I rummaged in my pockets for cigarettes, all the time staring deep into his eyes, then I asked him for a light. I was in that sort of mood and wasn't surprised when he fired that 'gun' of his and lit the damn thing for me. I allowed a smile to spread across my face as I slowly reached towards the glove compartment. Suddenly he snatched the keys from the ignition and threw them across the street. I looked at MoPic again as if to say what the fuck was that about? But still he didn't say a word. He just climbed out of the car and started wandering up and down the street looking for the car keys, while I took his place behind the wheel. Me and Sonny argued for what seemed like hours, screaming at each other at the tops of our voices, neither of us listening to the other, or even remembering what the argument was about. He didn't want a spliff, or a pipe, or any crack, he just wanted his money. He kept going on about it until finally I handed the wad back to him, every penny of it.

He snatched it out of my hands, counted the money, then silently stepped out of the car and left. He shoved the 'gun' in his back pocket and disappeared into the night, just like that. I didn't give him a second thought. I built myself a spliff, totalled up what money I had left and waited for MoPic to find those fuckin' keys. I was ready to go home.

Ellie

As far as we can help it we always keep Debbie away
from our drugs. We just couldn't afford to let her see
anything like that. I've had so many people tell me that
if you let your kids see you using then they won't do it
themselves later. I think that's the biggest load of shit
I've heard. I know how stressed I get when I'm sitting
there watching people do it in front of their kids; blood
all over the place, an hour-and-a-half trying to get a
vein! That's complete and utter shit. It's bad enough for
adults, never mind children.

That fuckin' Sadie lets her young 'un go in there, get
the foil and she'll roll out a tube pretending it's a
tooter. Sadie just sits there watching. I've had to tell
people, 'I can't tell you what to do in your own house
but if you do have a smoke can you please send Debbie
out to play?' Then I've gone up there another day and
there they are tooting away in front of her. They just
don't care. I can't trust them for things like that. They
say that Debbie can go round there and play any time.
Yet even though we dig our smack and they smoke
theirs, I still can't trust them not to do it in front of
her. It's horrible 'cause Debbie ends up with no one to

play with and I feel like a snob.

Debbie isn't daft though. If we go into the kitchen sometimes we'll say, 'Hang on, Debs, me and Lance are just going to do something which you're not allowed to see. So if you hang on and listen out for the door we'll only be a few minutes.' She *has* asked and we've always said we're just smoking some of those funny cigarettes. But she hears other people talking, she knows the word 'drugs', she's not stupid. She's only a kid and does pick things up from people but that doesn't mean we have to ram it down her throat. In anticipation of her asking anything we always tell her it's special tobacco. She accepts that. She also knows it's a grown up thing and it's not to be talked about, you know. But that can't go on for ever, can it?

That's one of the reasons we stopped people using here because it doesn't matter how many times you tell them not to leave foil, or the cap, or anything at all lying around, it still happens. Debbie will come in saying, 'Look what I found in the bathroom,' and she'll be holding a fuckin' works or something.

I can remember when she was a baby and someone was having a dig at my house. I made sure that everything was cleared away but they still dropped something on the floor, a fuckin' blue needle, the same size as we use. The next thing I know Debbie is crawling about on the floor with it in her mouth. That was it. No more in my house! You've got to draw a line, haven't you?

Maureen

I remember the first lick I ever had, it was brilliant. It made me feel like I was on top of the world, like I was stood on everyone's head. I felt like a really nice person you know, really mellow and loving towards everyone. I wish I could feel like that all the time but it just didn't last long enough. After that first lick I was sort of pleading for some more, then I was on my hands and knees looking for crumbs. It was mad.

The first time I got it off a friend. I was really wary because I'd heard about it but it was still new to me. All my friends said it was good stuff; they used it all the time. I thought I'd try it 'cause they said I wouldn't get a bad trip off it. We didn't have a pipe so we used a drinking glass with baking foil over the top. It was good but it should've lasted much longer. It's a good job I didn't pay for that first one otherwise I would've thought it was a waste of money, but obviously because I liked it I wanted more. If you could have a big dose that lasted in your system for about three months that'd be well worth it. In fact, we should be born feeling like that for life. It gave me a right happy buzz but after about ten minutes I was fed up and wanted another one. And when it got down to the last rock I was practically begging my mate for it. I was being nice to her but really I felt like being violent to make sure I got another one, but I couldn't. The rock made me feel too nice. I didn't have as much as her, she was into it more than me, but she did share the last rock with me.

I've been trying to give it up since then because one time, after I'd smoked a load of rock with this guy, I had to pay for it in kind. That did my head in. He let me have as much as I wanted but I didn't enjoy it 'cause I knew how I had to pay for it. I didn't even like the man. It was just because I was wired. I've not bothered with it since then. I mean, I'm not going around shagging everyone for it so I'm trying to stop.

Lanre: Fear of Dying

It's about 7.15 on the evening of my thirty-fifth birthday. I'm lying on my bed watching the Channel 4 News and steadily smoking my way through a biscuit tin of wicked home grown. The ganja is awesome, a hybrid of that skunk weed just come over from the 'Dam, and I'm so totally stoned I feel like I'm suspended in a state of pure levitation. My girl is in the bathroom doing her own thing. When she's finished she comes back into the bedroom to sort me but I'm so wasted I can hardly lift myself up to the occasion. So, nonchalantly, I throw an arm over the side of the bed exposing my veins for her, but it's not enough. She's already feeling a rush coming on as her own hit begins to take effect, so the very last thing she needs is for me to screw it up for her. 'Will you sit up and pay attention?' she hisses at me through clenched teeth. 'And why don't you use a bloody tourniquet or something?'

SIT UP! PAY ATTENTION! USE A TOURNIQUET!

She knows I hate this fuckin' ritual and want nothing more to do with it. But she also knows that secretly I still crave the buzz; that all my protestations and promises to one day quit this bullshit are absolute non-starters. At the end of the day I'm still just as addicted as I ever was. She reckons my phoney 'resistance' is all part of the process and serves only to prolong my anticipation and therefore heighten the buzz.

'It's gonna take a lot more than promises,' she sneers at me, yet again. 'The fact is you're just as caught up in all of this as I am. You're a fuckin' junkie and that's all there is to it!'

Secretly I know she's right but worse still is that smug-arse look she adopts when *she* knows she's right and I'm halfway in agreement with her.

She slides the needle smoothly, expertly under my skin. There is no mess, only a slight stinging sensation as she probes for the vein then draws blood up through the needle and into the syringe. She presses down lightly on the plunger to check that everything is correct then, satisfied, pushes it all the way home, slowly and without fuss, until all the cocktail of heroin and cocaine is flushed into my body. Almost immediately, even before she's pulled the needle out of my arm, I can feel a tidal wave of pure pleasure rushing through my veins. I feel joy teasing at my toes, my finger tips, swelling up in my groin and tingling the base of my spine. I can feel it tearing through the back of my throat and numbing my windpipe as it rushes up into my brain. Pins and needles savage the top of my skull; my brain feels like it's about to explode. My head is booming, heart pounding, and the pressure on my lungs is almost unbearable. It's as though a lid has been placed over my windpipe, making it impossible to breathe.

Feels like I'm on a roller-coaster falling out of the sky. Twisting and turning, tumbling through the air. The wind is beating a double-bass rhythm against my ear-drums as I hurtle towards the ground. Every fibre of my body is braced against impact.

Then just before touch-down, I'm swooping back up again, soaring higher and higher. But the ascent, now synchronized with my blood pressure, appears to have no end: the higher I climb the faster the blood is propelled through my veins as my breathing becomes shallower. This is too much, too soon – I can't take it! Now the panic sets in and I can't sit still for worrying. Yet at the same time I dare not move for fear of pushing myself completely over the edge. I sit down, stand up, then sit down again in the middle of the bedroom floor. 'Try to relax your mind, your body will follow,' I tell myself. But as I begin to let go of my fear I get a feeling of *déjà vu*, like I've been here before.

I remember London. MoPic and that fuckin' crack pipe. He told me later that I was only hyperventilating, that I could've saved myself a heap of trouble if only I'd used a paper bag. That's it, I know what to do! I need a paper bag. The trick is to cover your nose and mouth with the bag and re-inhale the breath you've just exhaled. That way your lungs don't take in any fresh oxygen so eventually they calm down and you can breath again as normal. So I jump up and hurry into the kitchen desperate to find a paper bag but suddenly my heart takes a lurch, as though finally it's about to give up. I fall to my knees, my hands clutching my chest, fighting to catch my breath. My girl rushes to my side and throws her arms around my shoulders. She's trying to calm me down, trying to reassure me that everything is gonna be okay. But I don't have time for this. 'GET THE FUCK OUT OF MY WAY WOMAN! I NEED THAT PAPER BAG!' As I'm rummaging through cupboards and drawers, searching frantically for this essential piece of life-saving equipment, thinking that every second is my last, my eyes begin to re-focus, my head clears, and whilst my heart continues to pound, I feel as though I am regaining some sort of control. I look to my girl for a hug. We come together and embrace. But I'm holding her off a little so she doesn't damage my still delicate chest. She turns her back on me, sulking. Not to worry, she doesn't understand. Well how can she understand, what is she to do when I continuously stick my arm out for more, for yet another snowball, another attempt to do the job properly?

Giant

You see, the dangers of being a junkie are not just about overdosing or even getting busted by the police. Society marginalizes you so much that you stand out as a target, a non-person, for anyone to do as they want with you. So you've got to watch out for yourself all the time. It's not right. Anyone can say what they want, do what they want, and you always have to defend yourself against it. Society has branded you a fuckin' dirty junkie. How can you live a life like that?

Just the other day I arranged to spend some time with a friend in Halifax so I was walking over to my mother's house to borrow her car. I got as far as the BMW garage on Oak Lane when these fuckin' Asian guys leapt out on me. The girls in the refuge across the road saw it all happen and phoned the police but they couldn't get there for another forty-five minutes, so I went in to wait for them and cleaned myself up.

Basically what happened was that as I walked up the hill these blokes jumped me. I don't know how many of them there were but they went absolutely apeshit. They were using my head like a football. I'm not into fighting and I don't know how to fight. I don't want to know

118

either, so I just curled up and tried to protect myself. I managed to grab hold of one bloke's jacket, whilst his mate was pummelling into me, and asked him, 'Why are you doing this? If you don't stop you're gonna kill me and then you'll get fastened up for life. Is that what you want, a life sentence?'

He just screamed at me, 'Get off me jacket! Get off me fuckin' jacket!' His mate had a few more kicks at me then they both ran away. That's when those women from the refuge came over. I've got lumps and bruises all over my body and everything seems to have gone blurred and slowed down. Obviously I couldn't use the car after that so I phoned my mate in Halifax to come and pick me up.

I've still got no idea what it was all about. I'd just had a dig and was feeling quite pleasant. I was going up to my mother's but I missed the bus. It was one of them scenes where you're running after the bus, banging on the side, hoping the driver will hear you and stop, but he drove off. So I thought to myself, 'Fuck it. It's only twenty minutes, half-an-hour tops, I might as well walk it up there.' It all happened so fast. They were calling me, 'Ya dirty fuckin' junkie!' My head was throbbing, that's why I told them that if they didn't stop they'd kill me. I've been up all night thinking about it, wishing I could fight, but I'm not into violence. The worst thing is not being able to talk about it. If I'd told any of my mates they would've gone looking for them and then there would've been a blood bath. What's the use of that?

I read an article in the *Telegraph and Argus* about the

prostitutes. The vigilantes have got them on the move again. They're giving the girls on the beat a load of hassle and wanting to move them down to Valley Road where there's no houses or anything. And the police are saying, in fuckin' *huge* capital letters, that they're aware of the problem but still they don't do anything about it. I mean, where the fuck were they when those bastards jumped on me? It was the vigilantes who did me. I don't know it for sure but they see me walking about, they know who I am, what I do and all that . . . That's what I mean about being a target. I go about my life trying not to upset people, minding my own business, doing my own thing. I just get on with it. But when they start pointing their finger you've got to defend yourself.

The girls in the refuge said the security man from the BMW garage came out as well, had a look then walked away. He *must've* seen me getting that beating. I was aware of a car pulling up too, he slowed down, had a look, then he fucked off as well. And all the time I was getting a fuckin' hammering. They were really going for it, both of them kicking my fuckin' head in. It's a bit upsetting when I think about it.

But I'm not really so bothered about the beating, who's come out on top, who's first, and all that. Like I said, I'm not into fighting. What does bother me is the fact that I was brought up in Manningham and I still can't get any peace. I've lived and worked here all my life, got into all sorts of problems and I still love the place. I love everything about it; the trees, the buildings, even the people. I've been around the world, visited so many different countries and always come back to

Manningham. It's just a shame I had to come back to this. It's so fuckin' sad. Manningham is the best part of Bradford but I can't enjoy it any more. That's what's distressing me. It's like the thing I love most is turning against me. And all because of those fucking vigilantes. Who the *fuck* do they think they are? Is being a vigilante any better than being a junky?

I'm fuckin' gutted. I'm supposed to be a great dad today. It's my daughter's birthday, I'm supposed to be going for a meal at 4 p.m. I'm just absolutely gutted. It's knocked the fuckin' shit out of me. It really has.

Lanre: Drugs Bust

So there's me back on the street with the hustlers, the dope fiends, and the police informers. Out of the hole and in one hell of a rush to set the record straight.

Someone grassed me for sure and I wanna to do for them as they did for me, as *she* did for me. I wanna to find that Yasmin – fuckin' Judas!

First stop was the Sunlight cafe on Manningham Lane. We knew it as Parker's, after the geezer who first opened the place then closed it down years later when he was busted on a drugs and 'use of premises' charge. Used to be one of two cafes on the Front Line, with business alternating between them, depending on which one was in favour and the amount of police activity in the area. Then, when the Young Lions was busted a few months later, Parker's re-opened under new management and for 'business as usual'. Today, after half a dozen change-of-hands and everywhere else either closed down or busted, Parker's remains the sole meeting place for the young hustlers and is drumming up a wicked business. So if you wanna score, you have something to sell, or just wanna hang tough with the action, then Parker's is the place to be. Everyone knows about that little gold mine: who's who, who thinks they're who, and who isn't.

Yasmin Bakatullah was nobody special, at least not until she fucked me off to the slammer. Like most of us she too was drawn to the Sunlight like a moth to a flame and was there again that night hunched around a steaming mug of coffee and looking something like a fugitive. As usual the cafe was jumping. People hung around in groups, their heads locked in conversation, or sat by themselves eavesdropping, tuning in to a re-run of that day's events. The news was about me getting busted: What happened? Who put me down?

Yasmin just sat there in a lonely corner doing her best to avoid all eye contact. Then I burst in through the door and suddenly all the talk came to a full stop.

Heads turned in my direction but I blanked them all and went straight for Yasmin's jugular. I had this two-handed death-grip around her throat so fuckin' tight she rushed through all the colours of the rainbow before someone managed to prise me off her.

I was seething. I wanted to tear the bitch's head off, fuck her up like she'd fucked me, but it was useless. I couldn't do anything there, not with everybody watching me like that. I had to get a hold of myself. So I barged my way out of the cafe, leaving in exactly the same way as I'd entered, a silence trailing behind me that some sad bastard had nearly died for. That fuckin' Judas could wait, she was going nowhere.

I didn't see anything of her for quite a while after that, it was as if she'd disappeared. But what did I care?

As far as I was concerned she was a real danger and the further she stayed away from me the better.

But I should've known, Bradford is too small for her to have dodged me completely – the place reminds me of a goldfish bowl sometimes. They often say up here that if you stand at one end of the city and sneeze, some friendly chap at the other end will offer you his handkerchief. Well I don't know, maybe it was a sneeze or maybe it was just one of those bad vibes you get whenever you're within the vicinity of a grass. But one afternoon I was in the cafe when suddenly Yasmin appeared at the door.

She didn't see me, she just waltzed in, ordered a coffee and sat down at the same place as I found her the last time. Looked like she was waiting on someone.

I'd hoped that she might even have gone and dug a hole for herself and didn't reckon on the fact that she had to score her drugs from somewhere. Meanwhile she just carried on as normal, putting up an innocent front: 'Who me? What did I do?'

Then we locked eyes and immediately she's starting the water works again. Swearing on everything holy, on every member of her family, that she knew nothing and had nothing to do with the plot against me. I could feel fury welling up inside of me, just itching to straighten out that frilly lip of hers. But there's something dark and depressing about a woman's tears which works against me every time. Doesn't matter who she is or what she's done, once I see those tears I'm always eager to forgive and forget. And then other times, God forbid, they're pushing and pulling, taking advantage of the slack, until they've just about driven me crazy. The next thing I know, tears or no tears, all the love is gone and I'm forgetting my manners.

I'm not really into any of that misogynistic stuff but listening to Yasmin's bullshit again just about freaked me out. I couldn't believe what an actress she was.

And those tears cascading down her cheeks like it was *me* who'd done her wrong! She claimed the set up was down to some Asian guy, a smack dealer, who'd been busted a couple of weeks earlier, then grassed on everyone to save himself. Only this wasn't your average junkie doing the big squeal to get his charges dropped. This guy was a regularly paid informer, a wannabe super-grass – practically a cop like them, just that they hadn't given him a uniform yet. This motherfucker was the type who would've marked you out to the Gestapo with a cross on your back; who delighted in those midnight assignations and passed over enough information to put his competitors away for years. This guy's relationship with the Old Bill was a closed shop and guaranteed their protection.

Although he was busted every now and again, not only to disguise his grassing but also to keep the bastard in line, he was one of the police's greatest weapons in their 'war against drugs'. So they needed to keep a tight grip on him and whenever he got too bolshie they'd give him a tug. Unfortunately his last bust was out of town, where he wasn't known and protected.

So he spent that weekend in the police cells withdrawing and sweating like the pig he was. Monday morning his 'protection' arrived and the case didn't even get as far as the charge desk. They whisked him out of there, fed him full of heroin, then put their heads together to plot a new line of strategy. Well, so be it. But I don't go for shit like that.

But the Judas swore blind it was true. She claimed this guy wanted an ounce of cocaine, wanted it washed up too.

But knowing he couldn't come to me direct he went through her. She charged him over the odds, almost twice the actual price, then phoned me to sort it. Within minutes he was back with the money plus a bonus for herself! It was unbelievable. But what I didn't know was that the whole thing had been planned and financed by the police. I just thought Yasmin wanted an ounce of cocaine and seeing as I knew her well enough, I trusted her. Today, though, I find it almost impossible to trust in anything. The minute you begin trusting or believing in someone you leave yourself wide open.

So we put Yasmin on hold for a while and concentrated our efforts on the bigger grass. If what she said was true then we were gonna put that fucker down, like a dog!

We discovered that as well as being a grass he also worked as a middle-man, a runner, for a bunch of smugglers based in Pakistan, on the North-West Frontier bordering Afghanistan. They call that region No-man's-land, a place where the Pathan, and their mujaheddin cousins, when they're not mercilessly whipping the Russians at war games, are busy in the manufacture and world-wide distribution of arms and top class heroin. Here in Bradford the Pathan were supposed to have a fearsome reputation (albeit created by themselves) but if we allowed talk like that to stand in our way then we might as well have just laid down for them. It's the difference between busting balls or having your own balls busted.

To us small-timers all that international shit was obviously big business and supposedly out of our league. That is until we discovered that he was also dealing heroin of his own; a scam he worked on the side and didn't share with his associates.

His kudos was sky-high on the street, since he was one of the few who could boast, with any honesty, that his gear came 'direct'. But as well as disguise, the street also provided him with the information which he traded to the police. His international connections, which normally put him out of our reach, were useless once he was back on home turf, because dealing smack to the locals made him one of us: a street hustler and just as vulnerable.

We knew the Asians had control of the heroin business and had done since their arrival in Bradford. But for some reason we must've allowed our prejudices to mess up our judgement 'cause we just couldn't imagine how they'd organised such an operation, and so successfully at that. Most of them were still our punters and that fuckin' grass was right in there with them! We must've blown more than just a few brain cells trying to work that one out, and thinking up ways to stick one on him.

But we wanted more than that, much more.

As a city on the verge of a nervous breakdown,

Bradford often takes refuge in the day to day mismanagement of its multicultural diversity. The relevant authorities love to boast about how the city has resolved its racial differences and now survives on a heterogeneous diet of tolerance and understanding, hence the slogan 'Bradford is Bouncing back.' But the whisper of friction that exists between the Blacks and Asians is not always so skilfully muted; when it does blow it often blows at a full scale crescendo.

Both communities balance their lives on the lower rungs of the social ladder, so it's inevitable there'll be some stamping on heads as one group tries to rise above the other. Like the time when three Asian guys walked into the Mayflower Club, pulled out a gun and shot, at point blank, two black guys then calmly walked out again. One guy had a knee-cap blown away, the other was hit in his arm. All hell broke loose inside the club and somewhere amidst the screaming, the cussing and the general panic, threats were being hurled about. But as usual nothing came of it.

A few weeks later, long before the mayhem had faded from our memories, there were more reports of gun shots. This time in the Sugar Cane Club. A young Asian guy, not much older than school age, took a Magnum hand gun and shot a black kid in the head. They'd been arguing over a game of pool.

The bullet went through the side of his head and came out of his arm.

Miraculously he survived – as did the shooter after receiving a near fatal beating.

Both were taken to hospital suffering serious

wounding to the head and upper body. After more threats and empty promises both incidents were lost in the history of Bradford's good race relations. On the Asian Front Line the shooters were applauded as minor celebrities and probably gained enough kudos to keep the flame burning in every Asian bosom for many years to come.

Other times the Black and Asian youth co-existed with an almost paranoid complicity. They had their Front Line, we had ours, and that's how we liked it: segregation by consent. We black boys had ganja and cocaine whilst the Asians peddled the big 'H'. Only, heroin wasn't so big anymore on account of charlie over-running the scene. Heroin still carried the swing and it seemed to me like suddenly everyone was a junkie, all of them stealing and cheating to support their habits. But the drug of choice now was crack cocaine. Coke. Rock. White. Stones. Charlie. Charlie was bigger than all of us and was set to dominate. That's when the shit really hit the fan and everyone got into it and the dynamite high they got in return. Hustlers, blaggers, prostitutes, pimps, all coming off one high and on to another. All of them scheming, stealing, cheating, even shooting at each other, just to get a piece of the action. But the buzz is only sweet the first couple of times out, then you're hooked and chasing that first high. Every subsequent buzz is a sad reminder of the original.

That's how it works – the donkey and the carrot scenario – and how the dealers squeezed the punters 'til they coughed up £25 for another rock. Then, when crack-cocaine became the absolute, the violence started.

In a situation like that there's got to be winners and losers, so the people firmed up, moved as a crew, to protect themselves and their business. And if any one of them fell by the wayside, or into the hands of the enemy, then they could always take that big step and grass. Just so long as they saved their own skins first.

It was crazy. Everybody grassed on everybody; best friends robbed best friends; mothers shopped their sons or shot at their neighbours. No-one got away unscathed. That's where our man came in, going on like he was the fuckin' Old Bill or something, as if he was fire proof. When all the time he was simply fuckin' us all in the arse.

So yeah, we wanted to make a BIG example of him. We wanted to show that nonce where it was really at; that we were one firm not to be fucked with.

It was Mikey who came up with the plan, he liked to play things that way. 'Just leave it to me,' he insisted, 'I'll sort it.' He wanted to kidnap the man, take him into the woods and beat him to death.

Or at least so near to death that when he recovered he'd think that we really went out to kill him. 'He'll realise then just how fuckin' close he was.' I thought it was quite an interesting idea, although personally I was more in favour of fixing him up with a wrap of battery acid. But, anyway, I let that one slide and looked forward to watching Mikey at work. Mikey was gonna take care of everything and let us know when he was ready.

By this time Yasmin was well out of the picture. The last I heard of her she was working the beat, so at last I felt that Parker's wasn't out of bounds; I could go into the cafe without fear of being shown up and losing control. Maybe I was expecting too much . . .

One day my mobile rang; it was Layla. 'Yeah, what do you want?'

'It's me, Layla,' she answered. 'What're you doing?'

'Nothing much, just eating some food. Why, what're you doing?'

'Well I'm laying in bed with my legs open, waiting for you,' she replied. 'D'ya wanna come over and do me a favour?'

I laughed. What is this? I'd had enough of punters and their bloody favours. I needed to be left alone, I had other stuff to think about. 'Oh yeah?' I said. 'Where's Brandy? Why don't you get *him* to do you the favour? I'm busy.'

'I'm finished with him. We've had a big fight and he's moved back home. Why don't you come over, bring some rock with you and we can have some fun.' I laughed again, maybe because I knew just how serious she was. She'd been at this all night, phoning me, trying to get cocaine on a promise.

When I knocked her back the last time she started coming on with this sex thing, describing what she would do for me, how I could have anything I wanted, absolutely anything. I wasn't interested.

Twenty minutes later she phoned back offering even more kinky sex for less cocaine than she asked for originally. But I was getting pissed off now 'cause she was putting me off my supper. So I made some tut-tut sounds and hung up. I knew the game perhaps even better than her. Brandy had probably put her up to it, maybe he was hiding in the bathroom or even under the bed, waiting to catch me in some compromising situation. Then he'd think he'd got one over on me and try taxing a lump of crack. Sad bastard.

But that's how it was. Everybody was trying to get something over everybody else. Losing themselves to crack. They thought they could handle it but Charlie don't give a shit. Not for anyone. Then, when he's got them boxed in, the women end up having to sell themselves.

Most dealers, with never a thought of turning down free pussy, would leap in with their dicks on fire – some of them even burning themselves in the process. I remember that pretty little Lolita tempting every last grain of cocaine out of my pocket so fast I didn't even have time to get a hard on. Layla and Brandy were typical. 'Crack makes me feel so randy,' she once told me. 'I always need good sex after a pipe. But Brandy hogs it all to himself and gets really paranoid thinking that someone's watching him or trying to get into the house.' They'd argue, fall out, then buy their own rock without the other one knowing and smoke it all to themselves. It made no difference to me. I'd be selling twice as much at twice the speed. Some nights they'd spend up to £200 each. I know he got his money from dealing smack but God knows where she got hers from.

About a week after Layla's call I was in Maggie Mays having a drink with Lorraine, who was over from

Huddersfield surreptitiously dealing crack to the locals.

The music was so loud we were having to use sign language to follow our conversation. I had a new boy, Raz, at the bar discreetly dealing to those we knew and trusted, with Greedy standing by. Usually Greedy worked the Front Line by himself but the word was that Raz has been boasting and showing off his money, so Greedy was watching over him. If he didn't shape up then he was out. The paradox about our business was that we had to keep quiet about it.

We wanted people to know we were in business but at the same time we didn't want them to know. We had a product to sell but couldn't tell anyone about it for risk of getting busted. We couldn't advertise it or talk about it yet we wanted people to buy it from us. Seemed like an impossible task but in actual fact it was a business like any other business and sold just as well if not better. Cocaine is virtually the single most expensive commodity in the world today. Far more expensive than gold or even platinum. I used to explain it to Raz, that there are countries whose whole national economy is based on the exportation of cocaine, whether legally or illegally, so we were doing nothing more than getting a slice of the cake for ourselves.

I got the wink that Raz was doing okay when suddenly I was distracted by this guy leering at me from across the room. He sat with a group of Asians around a table laden with drinks, talking in a language I didn't understand. But for some reason I knew their conversation was about me. One of them, stocky, with a pock-marked face like it'd just been sand-blasted, deliberately searched me out, looked directly at me then quickly turned away again. In that instance, that fraction of a second, I knew he was the grass! I couldn't believe it, the fuckin' grass sitting right there, just a few feet away from me and behaving like he might even have sussed it himself. How could I be sure it was him? I'd never even seen the bastard before.

But there was no need. I could feel the hairs on the back of my neck standing on end and a charge of electricity surge through my body.

I knew it was him, I just fuckin' knew it. Then, without even being aware of it, I was rising out of my seat, knocking tables over, spilling drinks into Lorraine's lap and reaching for a bottle, a heavy glass ashtray, anything . . . I was gonna take him right there and then. It was like remote control, like I was on autopilot.

But then someone had hold of my arm and Greedy was screaming into my face, forcing me backwards against the wall. Then they were both on me, dragging me, pulling me, running me out through the door, and all the time Greedy was shouting in my ear, 'Leave it, man, leave it. C'mon, leave it. We've got him already, don't fuck it up!' Lorraine, puzzled, gathered up our coats and ran after us, instinctively not wanting to be left behind. Outside I was bent over double against the wall, swallowing big gulps of air, trying to clear the raging ocean in my head. And as people streamed out of the door, the pub emptying like a bomb scare had hit the place, the grass stood surrounded by his friends, keeping a guarded distance. In between the scattering crowd I could see his eyes wide open, his mouth opening and closing like a goldfish, like he was trying to say something. But he was hustled away by his friends who formed a protective circle around him, directing him towards his car. They were speeding off, effortlessly gathering speed, in a shiny, brand new, Mercedes.

The Monk

There is a saying, you know, that 'idle hands make mischief.' But I'm inclined to think that it's an idle brain that makes even more mischief. If you're just sitting staring at a blank wall doing nothing your mind begins to wander. It starts craving something to engage with, and it seeks pleasure. It wants to feast on something. And what it was used to, what it mentally feasted on before, was smack. So naturally it wants more. It wants to gorge itself on smack like it used to. And because our senses are the most powerful receptors of the subconscious thought, the brain starts sending out a message: 'I need some smack! Get me some smack! Smack! Smack! Smack!'

Sometimes I dream about smack and I know the next day I'm gonna have to go through the gauntlet again to find some. I'm gonna have to lie and cheat, steal from my friends and family just to get a wrap. Sometimes I dream about a £10 note. Nothing more, just a tenner, 'cause that's all it takes. But the worst thing is I never actually get the smack! I dream about it, hustling or stealing the money, I might even get the wrap, but then something always goes wrong. It's either I spill it or I get caught smoking it, whatever. I never manage to *do* the smack in the end. That must be the 'good' person in me, I suppose. The *real* me who doesn't use gear. It's like there's some kind of internal struggle going on, a fight between good and evil. Like you develop another limb, another being, that's like an extension of yourself. Just like women have an instinctive drive about giving birth and bringing up children. For junkies it's the same thing. There's a part of their brain that's wholly centred on getting smack. It's instinctive and there's nothing they can do about it.

I know some people who're even selling £5 wraps now and they're making heaps of money. That's just about the same amount of pocket-money the kids are getting nowadays, isn't it? Over in Allerton there's a lot of school kids using gear now. The youngest one I know is about thirteen years old. I don't know how much he's using and I bet his parents don't know either. But how the fuck is he gonna get off that? He's gonna be fucked up now for a long time. At least until the realisation dawns or he's used so much gear that he ends up topping himself. The sad thing is, at that early age he's still got a long way to go before the realisation *does* dawn on him. Maybe when he's forty years old he might be mature enough to grow out of it. But imagine that, forty years of hard-drug use! And that's not all, he's using crack, whiz, Es, you name it, he'll do it. It's become a way of life for him.

I don't get too obsessive about crack. It's not my thing. It don't serve my needs so I have no interest in it. I haven't had a rock for years now and if I did get one

I'd swap it straight away for brown. Even when I was using crack I never really liked it. It made me spew or go to the toilet. So really it was just a waste of time. And from what I've seen out there I'm fuckin' grateful too! It's a mess, a thousand times worse than smack.

To tell you the truth I don't know how I'm gonna get out of this habit. If people like Keith Richards can try blood transfusions and hypnotherapy and still fail then what chance have I got? I reckon it'll be when I'm completely ground down, when it's become too much hassle. I can go five, six, days now without having a toot then it's in my head again and I've just *got* to get it. That's when I get into the robbing and the cheating again. I have no choice. That's why I'm back at work. And I must admit I do feel better now that I'm working, even though I am still using. It's easier and I feel better for it. Even the hassle of getting up in the morning isn't a problem 'cause it becomes automatic after a while. My body wakes up at the same time every morning without an alarm clock.

Sometimes you think to yourself, 'I'll sell it and that way I can make my habit pay for itself!' So you start dealing but then something goes wrong. You get ripped-off, you lose your money, or you get kicked. BANG! Reality smacks you in the face and you're worse off than when you started. You've got no money and a bigger drug habit. Where do you go from there? You might even have charges against you and be facing a jail sentence.

Short cuts. They're all short cuts which you think are a means to an end, but because class A drugs are all back-to-front and upside-down, those 'short cuts' end up being a much quicker route to the bottom. I mean, how many short cuts can you take? You take so many and go so far you end up doubling back on yourself, or in jail, or dead! You never learn. In fact, every time we take a short cut and it goes wrong we should lose a limb. I wonder how long it'd be before we learnt then.

But I'm sick of being a criminal, you know what I mean? There's no future in it. Not at the level I'm involved in, just stupid things to survive. It's like doing a wrap just to get my body feeling right but not doing it for the buzz. There's no enjoyment in it any more.

I suppose it's a matter of choices. I believe we've all got choices and if someone really wants to stop then they will. They'll just give it up and stop right there. And them that don't, or claim that they can't, just don't want to. I really do believe it's as black and white as that. We all come up with excuses why we can't stop but there's only one really and that is because we don't want to. All the rest of it is rubbish.

I don't even believe it's the cold turkey that scares them, I think it's the coldness of reality; life without stimulants, having to face up to themselves. I mean, these people who're on like a couple of wraps a day don't really cold turkey, do they? I mean, not *really* they don't, it's just anguish, a temper anguish. Like mummy's got some sweets but you can't have them until after you've had your tea. You know what I mean? The pain is more in their heads than in their body. They're in pain and thinking to themselves that if they could just have a toot it'd sort them out. But that just emphasises the problem, knowing there's a simple remedy to stop it. Excuses, excuses, excuses.

Lanre: Robbery

I drove home to Bradford and didn't breathe a word about my near-death experience. In this business you talk about a fear of dying and there's some head-the-ball starts marking your card. Before long he's trying to do the job on you himself and then jumping into your shoes. So at 5.30 that morning I crept into town and went over to a girlfriend's house to get some sleep. I was knackered. My head was wrecked after all that bullshit with Sonny. I just wanted to fall into bed and snuggle up to someone warm and inviting.

By rights I should've been out on the street chasing up Mikey. I'd left him in charge of the business while I was away, but with only a half ounce of rock to sell it was pretty crucial that I got the new supplies to him. But, like I said, I was just so knackered. And besides, I really didn't want to spend the rest of that night fending off Mikey's questions and ducking difficult explanations.

I didn't want anyone to know about that incident with Sonny, I wanted to keep the details to myself. It was all too embarrassing for common knowledge.

It's not so much that you have to live a lie or cower

down behind the make-believe. After all those years on the street, wheeling and dealing with hustlers just as hungry as yourself, you learn very quickly to keep what you know to yourself. Experience teaches you when and where to open your mouth, what to say, and how to say it.

So you stay quiet and unassuming; you keep your head down, your eyes and ears open, and understand that what you *don't* know is not your business. Even I couldn't stand too tall without the fear of one of my own team players taking a shot at me – sometimes even literally. So you learn how to bullshit and play the game, but you gotta play to win 'cause second place don't count.

Dealing crack cocaine is easy, just about anyone can do that, but staying out there, alive and in profit, that's the challenge. Eventually somebody always comes sniffing around: an aggrieved punter, a junkie who reckons they haven't been 'looked after'. Then the Old Bill get wind of it and suddenly staying alive is paramount. The fact of it is you have to be lucky *all* the time whereas the cops, the wannabes, and the grass, need only to be lucky once! Life on the street is never anything but a gamble.

So I was at Mica's house trying to cool my heels before hitting the streets again, but as soon as she sussed out that I had cocaine in my pockets the girl was all over me.

I didn't even get a wink of sleep. So to avoid an argument I chopped off a little piece for her and ran myself a bath instead. Minutes later she followed me into the bathroom hassling for another piece . . . and another piece . . . until finally I couldn't take anymore. But then, just before I kicked off, there was someone hammering on the front door and I felt so relieved that I just flopped into the water. She stomped off downstairs, vexed at the interruption, only to discover it was her boyfriend with a car full of friends!

Mica almost had a fit. She was so petrified she couldn't open the door. So she ran back up to the bedroom, like a frightened squirrel, looking for somewhere to hide.

I was pretty freaked out myself. I'd been relaxing in the bath with no apparent reason for even being in her house and her boyfriend was on the doorstep demanding to be let in! Maybe I should've ducked out the back door, any sane person would've done just that. Instead I tried to calm her down so we could think of something. When that didn't work I had to accept there was no other choice but to let him in. What else could we do?

Her head was in bits and so was mine. I worried that if she delayed any longer the boyfriend would get suspicious and break the door down. Then he'd find me and there'd be no amount of explaining that would calm the situation. I tried to imagine the scene . . . but my imagination just didn't want to know.

So I called out to Mica *not* to open the door – at least not until I'd got some clothes on and prepared myself for whatever was coming next.

I heard slamming doors downstairs then raised voices, so I guessed she must've let them in already.

Mica was crying and screaming at someone. I heard more slamming of doors, more raised voices, then suddenly all hell broke loose. My instinct was to jump out of the bath and rush downstairs but I didn't move. I couldn't, it wasn't my business . . . not yet anyway. So I lay there, not moving, with the water up to my neck, straining my ears.

When I heard the sound of breaking glass and Mica shriek out in pain, I did leap out of the bath and dive into the bedroom to find my clothes. But I'd only got as far as the landing at the top of the stairs when I saw him dragging her by the hair across the hallway and out of the front door to where his pals were waiting for him in the car. Dripping wet and struggling into my jeans, I watched him from the bedroom window beat her with something as he dragged her across the garden; her bloodied mouth wide open in a silent scream.

It was my fault. I should never have been at her house in the first place. I knew I'd messed up and got myself into a no-win situation. I felt bad about the beating she took. I wasn't into any of that stuff myself, but still it wasn't my business and neither was I in a position to intervene.

It's a strange thing how sometimes Manningham appears to legitimize domestic violence. Of course that type of nonsense happens the world over, but in Manningham it is a daily occurrence. In fact, if I had intervened they most probably would've turned on me. So I think I did the best thing by staying out of sight. If the boyfriend had known I was there that would've been even more reason for him to beat her.

But there was also some selfishness on my part, too, since I was only at her house to rest up and recharge my batteries. As far as I was concerned she didn't even need to be home, I had my own door key anyway. And whatever went on between her and her boyfriend was their own business. My presence would've only exacerbated the situation when all I wanted was to be in and out of there as quickly as possible.

Very arrogant, I know, but that's how it is between dealers and punters. Even if she was a 'girlfriend' she was still only a punter, she was only business, and each of us was only looking out for ourselves.

I found Mikey holed up at his girl's house, smashed out of his face and climbing the walls. The half ounce of crack had sold out but the money didn't account. He'd obviously worried about this hole in our finances and had tried to score something to make up the difference but there was nothing to be had. No cocaine, no crack, nothing. West Yorkshire was suffering a drought – that's why I'd had to go to London. So that left Mikey in a bind. I found him huddled in a corner of the girl's bedroom, nodding. On the floor, scattered around his feet, were dozens of screwed up balls of tinfoil, all of them stained with the burnt up lines of heroin he'd been chasing. On the bed was a pile of money and a carefully documented list of sales. The business was exactly £425 short but according to his figures we'd come out evens and everything was in order! I didn't say a word, he wouldn't have understood me anyway, slumped there with his head between his knees. I just picked up the money and turned to leave but then I spotted a crack-pipe behind the door, loaded and waiting for him to blaze.

The man had spent my money on so much smack that he couldn't even finish off the crack he'd stolen from the business. It was a shame, a damn shame, but so fuckin' typical. If there's crack in the house you can guarantee it'll be polished off, no matter who it belongs to. No rock-head can resist it, they just can't sit still knowing there's a rock to be had and a buzz to jump on to. I felt more resigned than angry, but I remember promising myself, as I made my way out of that ambitionless hole, that first thing in the morning I'd sack them all.

Or instead of them I'd sack myself. It added up to the same thing, but as far as I was concerned they could stay exactly where they were, me and my business would walk away. Whatever part of it Mikey had controlled, even if it was only for one day, he was already bankrupt. So if he wanted anything more than that he'd have to find it for himself. I was on my own now.

Typical of those wannabe bad-boys who hit the Bradford Front Line in one hell of a rush to make a name for themselves, 'Rocco' Highsmith blasted on to the scene like a real sport. Straight away he and his crew were into everything: ripping off punters, hijacking drug deals, taxing the local whores . . . the man was a serious headache and caused a lot of aggro out there. Most of us saw that he had a problem more than an attitude so we tried to ignore him. But he still managed to keep us on edge, 'cause we all knew that one day somebody was gonna kick his arse, we just didn't know who.

Right from the beginning the man was trouble for me. As far as I was concerned he was an arsehole, especially after witnessing what he did to his girlfriend that night. But he still felt that I owed him something on account of me being at his girl's house in the first place. So never mind the fact that he'd smashed her face in and wanted nothing more to do with her, except on pay-day, I still had to deal with the effects of his bad mouthing me and demanding that I show him some respect. Yeah, right!

Meanwhile Rocco continued his psycho-dance through the Front Line and worked overtime on the reputation he'd carved out for himself. Everybody was pissed off with that nasty little fucker messing up their runnings but the crazy thing was he seemed to get away with it.

Then he got into a tangle with the twins, Dermont and Frasier, a couple of rip-off artists. The battle raged on for weeks until it appeared that both sides had lost interest.

One day Rocco, who appeared to have resolved his differences with the twins and whose trick was to get in real close and pally with his next victim, took Frasier, the younger twin, over to Leeds to sort some business. As soon as they landed Rocco turned round and robbed him. It must've been a real humiliation for Frasier, who thought he was pretty special since he always had his twin as back up, because not only did he lose his money and drugs but he was also held down whilst Rocco beat the shit out of him. Then he was left there half naked to walk the nine or ten miles back to Bradford. Nobody knew about that bust up until Frasier arrived home ranting and raving, swearing that he and his brother would hunt that psycho down and even the score.

Days later I was in Parker's having a bite to eat when the fall-out came down. I was only in the place five minutes when there was a big commotion at the bar. Rocco was raising hell. He pulled out a knife and stabbed it into the counter, splinters flew everywhere.

I just sat there with a mouth full of sandwich taking it all in, enjoying the show.

Then suddenly the twins came up from downstairs and rushed at him with a baseball bat. He didn't stand a chance. They beat him mercilessly and with such enthusiasm that even I, in my front row seat, felt the blows as they rained down on him.

It was like they really intended to kill the man.

As Rocco's legs buckled beneath him and he started to go down, Dermont held him up again so that Frasier could lash him some more. Then they dragged him out into the street and continued the punishment all over again.

Even with the door closed I could hear the thudding sound of the wood striking flesh, then bone, and the animal sounds from the twins as they worked him over.

By the time I'd finished my meal and joined the crowd outside the twins were long gone and Rocco was lying face down in a pool of blood. He was barely conscious but still refused to accept anyone's help. Even when someone offered to call an ambulance for him he groaned at them to fuck off!

He was not a pretty sight but still I couldn't help feeling a rush of satisfaction at seeing the little prick collapsed there, ground into the pavement like a dirty stain.

I bent down real close to him, so that nobody could see, and slipped a couple of rocks into his pocket. 'That's for the other night,' I whispered in his ear. 'Nothing personal.' It wasn't meant as an apology but I'm sure he got the message.

I don't remember much about that night of the robbery, it was a long time ago. Sometimes the memory comes shuddering back to me in snap shot mode, like a photographic negative upon which I have to work real hard to produce a positive thought. Some frames I remember all too clearly, like they were recorded only yesterday, whilst others remain blurred or scratched beyond recognition. Perhaps I've deliberately erased the details from my mind, after all it's not something I really want to remember. Although today, as I fix the memory to this page, it's as if I'm experiencing the damn thing all over again. Like some scabby old sore that's been reopened, healed over, and reopened again.

I remember I was staying with my boys that weekend and had just come downstairs from the bathroom when I spied three guys in the kitchen, three shapes like black cats in the shadows. I make a mental note as I continue on into the living room where Rocco is going on about the eighth he's ordered, about the two rocks he's bought and polished off already, about anything that'll distract my attention away from the kitchen.

Something is going on, I should've sussed it and been on my guard.

How many times have I warned Mary against allowing too many punters in at once? But she thinks she's safe. She has the situation under control because she knows Rocco, he wouldn't do her any harm. Besides she's a woman, isn't she? Her femininity is enough. So she wanders into the room full of joy and excitement at seeing him again, which is just enough to distract my attention even further.

Right behind her are the cavalry. They swoop into the room with their faces set, pulling weapons out from under their jackets. One of them pistol-whips Mary on the back of the head and she drops to the floor in a crumpled heap. Fuck her femininity! Shit, I should've known it'd be something like this. I make a move towards her. I want to pick her up and check that she's okay but my path is blocked by this runty little bastard brandishing a 12-inch screwdriver in his hand.

He only looks about seventeen years old, though he's trying to act big and tough for his friends. But he just can't stop his hands from shaking, so much so that the screwdriver is jumping all over my face. If he lunges at me now he'll probably miss. But nevertheless, this nervous, shit-scared little kid frightens me much more than the other one with the gun.

I try to force my way past him but another one, dark, thick-set, with a demented look in his eye, backs him up with a kitchen knife aimed at my throat.

This one is enjoying himself. He's even smiling, getting a big rise out of my hesitation. All I can think of is Mary lying there in a heap while they surround me with their guns, their knives and their fuckin' screwdriver.

They pause for a moment, as though they're taking stock of the situation, but then I realise it's the demented one, the one with the knife, who's holding them back.

He seems to be having some sort of silent dialogue with Rocco, urging him on, waiting for him to call the next move. But Rocco's face looks troubled like he can't quite remember what they'd rehearsed.

I'm praying to God that this is *not* the point where they'd planned to cut my throat. Rocco hesitates . . . takes a step forward . . . stops. Then, exactly like some tormented animal that has finally found its way, he suddenly rushes over and whacks me square in the jaw. The punch itself doesn't really hurt me but I still pretend like it's the worst possible thing he could've done and even fall back on to the sofa for effect. He appears suitably impressed then whispers in my ear, 'You know what that was for.' My mind whirls back to that day outside the cafe and suddenly I do remember, but instead of allowing this little shit to deny me such a wonderful memory, I'm trying to anticipate what's coming next. Mary picks herself up from the floor and comes to sit next to me on the sofa. She was only out for a couple of minutes but I swear it felt as though she'd been laying there forever. Even though she's completely revived now I still feel the need to shield her from these idiots. The desire to stand up and prove myself is so powerful it almost overwhelms me. I can see myself taking out Rocco with just one slap then using him as a battering ram to finish off the others. My Action Man fantasy is enough to give me a hard on but, like the good man said, 'He who fights and runs away lives to fight another day.' So I think I'll leave it out for the time being. Well, that's my excuse anyway.

Rocco and his boys begin a search of the room and find a sixteenth and a £100 rock that I'm saving for someone. The punter hasn't phoned back to confirm the deal yet so I guess it's a loss I can well afford, so they're welcome to it. There is no cash except for the £50 note Rocco paid me for a couple of stones earlier and which is still in Mary's purse somewhere in the kitchen. How does he miss that? And since he's reluctant to search upstairs for any real money I wonder if all this is worth their effort. I suppose only they can tell.

So now, having got all that there is to get – one fat rock – the gang make preparations to leave.

The lunatic with the kitchen knife stands at the window checking if their exit is clear; Rocco stands guard over me and Mary whilst the other two rush out the back door. Then 'Rambo' follows them out and last of all Rocco, walking backwards, keeping us in sight until the very last moment.

At last they're gone. But Mary and I stay exactly where we are, neither of us move for at least another ten minutes. Then gently I put an arm around her shoulder and pull her to me in a tight hug. I'm trying to comfort and reassure her that everything is okay now. It was me they came for; Rocco made his point and now he's gone. I doubt very much if he'll be back.

Well, that's what my body language is telling her, but inside I'm still reeling from the shock, the anger, and embarrassment of it all. I feel intensely disappointed and pissed off with myself. I'm not even sure now whether my hug does convey all that I want it to. Somehow I get the feeling that Mary's return hug is for reasons completely different to my own.

She keeps telling me over and over again, like she's trying to reassure herself, that I did the right thing, that there was nothing I could've done and it would've been stupid if I'd tried anything heroic. But that doesn't help. In fact I feel even worse because it's like she's the one protecting me. Now I can't even look at the woman so maybe I *should've* done something. Who knows, maybe one day I'll bump into Rocco again. As it is, we're told the little jerk left town immediately after the robbery. Someone's even reported seeing him on the remand wing at Armley jail. Well, whatever. If I never ever see the man again it'll be too soon.

Maureen

I went to this party the other day. It was only meant to be a two day thing but I got there a couple of days early and stayed the whole week. It was a crack party – rocks everywhere. There were so many dealers coming in and out, some of them even gave the stuff away for nothing. It was like, 'You wanna pipe? Yeah, well help yourself.' Everyone was sharing and passing the pipes around. The coke was just flowing; you couldn't get away from it.

I smoked so much I exhausted myself. I went right past the high and came back down again. But the next day was depressing; I had to cry myself past it. I couldn't go home because my son was there and that would've meant facing up to my responsibilities. I just couldn't be bothered with all that. I didn't want to face him when I was high and I couldn't be bothered when I was down. So I gave him some food and got him into bed. That wasn't fair really and it made me cry even more.

I was in a catch-22 situation. Where do I go from here? What do I do now? What I should've done was sort myself out. I should've spent time sitting quietly by myself and got my head together, but then the

154

selfishness set in and I ended up smoking even more crack. My excuse is I don't like sitting in the house alone and getting bored, but that isn't true really. At the end of the day I do like being on my own. I'm quite happy to just have a bath and sit at home watching the telly. I'm even happy just to go to bed. In fact, I prefer it really.

Maybe I'm trying to escape from myself. I always create distractions and do the opposite to what I really *should* be doing. It was that excuse again of being bored and not wanting to sit at home alone. So I went round and sat with a friend when really I didn't even want to be there. No, that's not right either. I *did* want to be with my friends but I knew that if I went and sat with them I'd end up smoking again – that's what it's like. The whole point was to get another rock to smoke. Once you start you can't stop. It's like you've got no control over yourself.

I knew exactly what was going to happen at that party, that's what I went there for, to smoke as much crack as I could – and that's exactly what I did. But the comedown was awful, the worst feeling in the world. There's nothing like it. It was gutting and made me feel sick. Not just physically sick but pissed off with myself as well.

When all the coke was done I couldn't communicate with anybody. People around me were saying, 'Look at her, she's gone on one of her trips.' I just thought 'LEAVE ME ALONE!' But I couldn't speak. The words wouldn't come out of my mouth. I didn't *want* to speak to anyone. I hated them.

I think it was the cocaine I hated really or maybe it was myself. I don't know. Obviously I do like people, I like their company otherwise I wouldn't have any friends. It was just this massive feeling of self-loathing and wishing that I'd never gone to that party in the first place. Then I got paranoid and started looking out of the window all the time. I think that was my insecurity and not feeling safe. It felt like there was something wrong or the place wasn't right, so I couldn't relax. It was really weird.

It's all different now though. I feel in myself I've got this amazing contentment that I've never had before. I still don't think that I could sit in a room where people are smoking though. I'd either have to walk out or join in with them. I don't think I'm strong enough to take them on yet. But I haven't smoked a rock for at least a week now. That's got to be good news, because I used to smoke every single night. If I could afford it I would've smoked all day, every day. But as I'm looking at it now I've seen certain people around me looking really bedraggled. I know I don't look a picture of health myself yet but I suppose I'll get better as I go along. I can see them now and they're beginning to stand out for what they really are. When you're on crack you just let your general health and appearance go. That's just how it is. You try to get on with your day to day life but you can't be bothered with how you look. You're so tired and run down all you want to do is sleep. The coke saps all your energy. That's how it works. The coke gets all its energy from you, then when you have no energy left it starts eating away at your body. That's why I'm trying to get away from it now. I don't need to look like that. Why should I? So far it's been a week . . . I'll see how far I can go without it.

Lanre: Drugs Bust

Almost one year to the day that Spencer went rushing off to join the big boys in London I got word, via the Front Line, that my old friend was back in town again. He was in trouble and wanted to see me. I had troubles of my own and was really not in the mood to deal with anyone else, but I went along to meet him anyway.

It seemed as though he hadn't changed much during the time he was away.

I expected him to return to Bradford even louder than he was before he left and boasting of his success, but I was disappointed. He looked haggard and so thoroughly strung out I thought he was gonna completely fall apart at any moment. He didn't waste time with pleasantries and asked me straight out if I'd take an ounce of cocaine off his hands. In fact he had three ounces left over from a deal that'd gone wrong and needed to sell them off quick before this 'bad man' caught up with him.

I told him I wasn't interested, but when he explained how this guy had already been to his house looking for him, had completely trashed the place and terrorized his family, I became interested and wanted to know more.

He said that in London it'd been even tougher for him to stay ahead of the game than it had been in Bradford. The competition was scarier; there was a new generation of kids coming up with no respect, no morals, not even the time honoured code of the street. So to give himself the kudos he felt he needed he went into partnership with a friend who played the bad guy and would set the punters trembling at the first sign of trouble. Spencer was the good guy to whom they paid their bill once they'd stopped trembling. For a short while everything was cool, the business began to flourish and at last they were able to relax a little and enjoy their profits. But then they started abusing their product and very quickly things fell apart. Their competitors, those same wannabe bad boys, stepped up to the mark and made their presence felt. Even the punters, who up until then had known their place, began to lose interest and eventually stopped dealing with them. Their output dried up and they lost business. As the situation tightened they began taking more chances and paying less attention to the levels of danger or the quality of the partners they ran with. Then Spencer was caught in a sting and it'd cost them over £10,000, every penny they had, to replace what they'd lost and set themselves up again. But it was too late; the competition had already sussed their weakness.

The second rip-off finished them off. And Spencer, unable to handle the fact that he'd screwed up yet again, escaped home to Bradford with the three ounces of cocaine and his partner, the 'bad man', chasing after him to claw back the money he owed.

We sat there together for another half an hour or so and he talked away every minute of it. About the terror that was bearing down on him, the deal he'd made, the money he owed, the stress he was under. He was laying on the pressure, trying to guilt-trip me into doing his bidding. The man talked so much it was painful listening to him. The words poured out of his mouth but they didn't mean a thing to me. They were just a lot of sad sounds coming from the most desperate of situations. He was obviously in a bad way and running scared but at last I began to see Spencer for what he really was: frightened and hating himself for not being stronger.

But still, why didn't I feel any sympathy for the man? Why couldn't I feel his pain? I mean, this is the man who bragged at every possible opportunity that he was the first crack dealer in town. The same man who dealt me in all those years ago and taught me how *not* to run a business.

He was in a position to set his own agenda, to make up the rules as he went along. So he should've known that the first rule of the game is to trust no-one; to pay off your creditors and never, ever, leave your debts hanging. You're always fair game on the street and you have to be stone-cold to survive. Nobody gives a fuck about you or the next man, not even the police. They couldn't care less who's 'doing' who just so long as someone gets done. They just wait until it's all over, until we've half killed each other, then bust whoever's still standing. Sometimes it's better to be the one heading for jail.

I didn't particularly want to get involved with Spencer again, especially since my sense of danger was ringing constantly like a burglar alarm in the night. Other people's bullshit always scares me more than my own but I grew up believing that you've got to look out for your friends. You've got to do for them as they do for you. So with that in mind we put our heads together and devised a plan. I'd wash up all three ounces of cocaine and instead of buying them from him we'd go out together and hustle them on the street. At least that way we'd raise the money needed to keep that head-hunter off his case and, who knows, maybe we could raise a little profit for ourselves too.

So that's how we played it; only it wasn't as simple as that. I should've known. With Spencer things are never so simple. To begin with, the powder was of such poor quality the first two ounces returned only 20 grams of crack between them and lost over £3,000. There was a slight improvement with the third ounce but altogether we were still £2,000 short of our target.

It was pathetic, but even worse was how Spencer had agreed to such a stupid deal. Then, as if that wasn't enough, I discovered he had absolutely no intention of going out and hustling the crack with me. His plan was to shack up with some fat girlfriend of his, piping and bonking the night away, whilst I did all the work.

I hit the roof! What was he thinking? And where did he get off taking out a stash for himself when he knew that even before we'd started we were already short of the target? Even under such 'life or death' circum-stances, as he described them to me, he still couldn't resist stealing something for himself just to show off to a girlfriend. The man was unbelievable. That alone should've alerted me to those damn alarm bells ringing inside my head but, just like Spencer, I guess I was also being held to ransom by the sweetness charlie had to offer. Even if I was only there for the money, at the end of the day I was just as much of a victim as he was.

I busted my balls all night for that fuckin' Spencer, even pushing his stuff before my own. But the punters were quick to suss out that the quality was down so they weren't biting as greedily as usual. I even had to tempt them further by giving away small discounts, but they are no fools. A crack head can tell the quality of a rock simply by looking at it. Then they'll take a hit and tell you how it was washed, who by, and anything else you want to know.

Get it wrong and you won't see them for dust. By the time daylight peeked through and I had Spencer up and ready to go, I still had rocks left to sell. But I couldn't cope with him hanging around me any longer, so I made up the shortfall in money from my own stash just to get rid of him. He could always pay me back later.

I literally had to drag him kicking and screaming from that woman's bed and down to the station. Then there was a brief struggle about me driving him to London rather than him taking the train. On top of everything else I'd done for him over the past day or so he could've walked down the motorway the wrong way as far as I was concerned.

I left him at the interchange with £4,500 cash in his pocket and a pained look on his face. It was about 6.15

in the morning and suddenly, as if to signal the start of a new day, my mobile started ringing . . .

At 7.30 p.m. I was tucked away in a 'safe' house washing crystal cocaine into crack and frantically organizing myself before going back out to work.

The mobile hadn't stopped ringing all day and was still squawking away in the corner of the room somewhere, but I had neither the time nor the inclination to deal with it.

But I still had a pile of complaints to deal with from a bunch of hard-arsed punters who were coming at me thick and fast, bitching about the shit I'd sold them yesterday. Some of them had scored two or three times and were so pissed off with the quality I had to re-wash what was left and reimburse them all. Funny how they complained only after they'd come down off their buzz and run out of money. I was being run off my feet, but at least the gear was still moving and at last the money was going into my pocket. Then, just before I'd run myself ragged, I got a phone call from Spencer. He'd just touched down from London and was on his way over to see me. The way I was feeling I knew that was a bad idea, but before I could suggest an alternative there was someone tapping out a secret knock at the front door and I just knew it had to be him. I couldn't believe it, what more did he want? Spencer ducked into the room waving his friend, a skunk specialist, in behind him. Both of them smiling like they shared some special secret and just couldn't wait to share it with me too. They were on their way over to Leeds they said, to 'cop some real drugs' and wanted me to go along with them. But surely Spencer had told his friend about the merry-go-round we'd been on all day yesterday and the miracle I performed with his dodgy cocaine. He should also have known not to bring strangers to the house. So if they were going to Leeds then why didn't they just bypass me and fuck off.

With his partner in jail, Spencer's friend now had to go and score his own dope. He wasn't too excited about going it alone so he'd asked Spencer to go with him. And with Spencer being on such a high after sorting that business in London he now thought that I was the man to hang with, so he called on me to tag along as well. I was reluctant to go anywhere near him – the man was a fuckin' liability – but he heaped so much praise on me, and his friend was so bloody deferential, I figured why not?

After such an unbelievably crap day perhaps the drive out of town would ease the stress I was feeling and turn my mood around. I insisted on using my own car, hoping the drive would help me to relax. We drove through the town centre, up Leeds Road and on to the Pudsey bypass, then, as we approached Leeds City Centre, Spencer suddenly got the idea that he'd like to find himself a new contact, someone better than the guys in London and, since we were in Leeds anyway, why not pick up a couple of rocks too?

Fuckin' Spencer! I could feel my mood wobbling again as my anger began to rise. He was saying 'why not this . . .?' and 'why not that . . .?' as though he'd only just thought of the idea!

We pulled into the Hayfield pub car park, Chapel Town. Spencer leapt out of the car and went over to speak to some shadow waiting for him on the corner and immediately we were besieged by a posse of teenybopper hustlers trying to sell us their wares.

I was surprised his friend didn't jump out after him. Wasn't he supposed to be meeting someone too? Instead he just sat there clinging to the seat behind me and scowling at the wannabees as they backed off and reclaimed their corners.

Minutes later Spencer rejoined us wearing a Cheshire cat grin on his face. He gave his mate a wink and pointed in the direction home.

Throughout the return journey the two of them huddled up close, deep in conversation, Spencer talking non-stop about some new business venture he was setting up. I was no longer interested in anything he had to say so I concentrated on the driving. But then he tossed a couple of rocks into my lap and asked me what I thought of them. If only I'd known what that bastard was getting me involved in I would've dumped those fuckin' rocks out of the window. As it was I told him what I thought he wanted to hear. He didn't say much but I guessed those rocks were samples for his new business, the idea that'd simply 'popped' into his head earlier. They were much better than the crap he'd brought up from London, but they had nothing to do with me so what did I care? Spencer was so chuffed with my opinion that he decided I should keep the rocks for myself. But, like I said, I wasn't interested in his business so only took one rock, pushed it deep into the pocket of my jeans, and passed the other one back to him. He seemed happy enough with that, so I carried on driving and left him to his excitement.

We were flying down Leeds Road when suddenly Mr fuckin' lightweight, who'd hardly dared to speak a word to me since we'd left Bradford, yelled at me not to drive through the City centre. But he was too late because we were already heading straight into town.

I didn't see what the problem was anyway. We only had two rock stones on board so where was the need for paranoia? I didn't like the man anyway, he just didn't appeal to me and was getting on my nerves. It really pissed me off that every time we saw a cop he'd get all jumpy and start acting like he was guilty of something, expecting me to get paranoid with him just because we were three black guys in a car. Like it was a condition that we should know our place, to refrain from doing our own thing and please everyone except ourselves.

Having a lightweight like him on board set my nerves jangling and spoilt what little buzz there was. Perhaps my bad luck day wasn't over yet. All I had to do was sit patiently and wait for something to happen. It didn't take long. Stuck at the traffic lights in the centre of town I spotted a police car file in behind us. I didn't pay it much attention 'cause at that time of night, when the whores are out and the night clubs are opening up, the cops are on top of everybody.

But when they followed us all the way to Manningham and up on to Lumb Lane I became a little more concerned and warned the others. There was still no real danger but the dipstick freaking out in my ear kind of upped the tension. I thought it was best to be ready so I dug that rock out of my pocket and put it in my mouth whilst keeping one eye on the situation behind me.

Spencer did the same, then checked that everywhere else was clean.

I looked to his friend but he played dumb, like 'what's the problem?' until the cops were bumper to bumper with us on Lumb Lane. Then he demanded to be dropped off at the cafe. I was reluctant to stop and let him off the hook but he insisted.

We continued on our way and, sure enough, once we were clear of the Front Line, they pounced.

I checked Spencer again, to be sure things were in order, then pulled over to the kerb. I couldn't believe it when 'Smith', the same cop who busted me just months before, stepped out of the police car and made his way over towards us.

Spencer looked apprehensive and straightaway I'm beginning to panic. I knew the police had nothing on me, so before I unlocked the door I checked him again. I had to be sure he knew the drill. He assured me that he was clean.

'Smith' was getting impatient. He started knocking on the window and tugging at the door handle but I was waiting on Spencer, so fuck him, he could wait.

Finally, when I was absolutely certain that we were both safe, I unlocked the door. Two cops immediately dragged me out of the car, handcuffed me and marched me over to one of three police vans that had arrived on the scene.

I complained and kicked up as much fuss as possible but it was just the same routine as the old days: two black guys arrested; two thousand cops to deal with the situation. I didn't see Spencer again until well after I was released.

In the police station I emptied my pockets and gave my details to the desk sergeant. Although I had no idea what we'd been arrested for, I really wasn't too worried. I figured I'd be out in an hour or so anyway. I didn't know that Spencer hadn't been arrested with me and wasn't even in the station. I just did as I was told, expecting to be released soon. The sergeant didn't appear too concerned either, so I took my cue from him.

It was all a simple misunderstanding. The car hire firm had reported the car to the police because the lease hadn't been paid that week. So effectively I'd been driving a 'stolen' car. Secretly I was shocked, and angry, although the sergeant only saw my surprise and my willing to make amends for my mistake. My cash was right there on the counter but he wasn't impressed. I was too late for that.

Besides, the rental manager was so beside himself with anger he wanted both drivers prosecuted and his car returned immediately.

What he didn't know was that I *had* paid for the car that week, just as I did every week. I gave my man the money for the rental, and any other necessities, and he was supposed to bring back a receipt. Obviously he'd messed up on this occasion and didn't tell me anything about it. There was nothing I could do about that now and I'd have to deal with him later.

But hours later, instead of being released as I expected, I was charged with handling a 'stolen' car and for possession of crack cocaine, which they claimed was found in the glove compartment during a search of the car.

I thought they were trying to trick me into something and almost laughed in their faces. What were they talking about? In the interview room 'Smith' produced a rock from its clingfilm wrapping, placed it on the table in front of me and talked about sending it off to some laboratory for testing. A quivering knot of apprehension grew inside of me. I could feel his eyes searching my face for a reaction, anything that would confirm his suspicions. The man had to be crazy if he thought I was gonna fall for something as fucked up as that. I didn't believe a word of it. How did I know that rock wasn't something he'd laid on himself?

I was confused but hoped to God my face didn't betray anything. That bastard was getting nothing out of me. I still had my own rock in my mouth, under my tongue where I'd carried it throughout the body search, in and out of the cells, and was determined to take it back out with me too. So there was no way he could've found anything in my car, not unless . . .

But that was impossible. Absolutely no fuckin' way. Spencer would never pull a stunt like that, surely?

So there's me in the cell again with a mattress and a blanket, staring up at the graffiti some joker had managed to 'scribe on the ceiling and thinking about the mess Spencer had got me into; that I'd got myself into.

Must be at least fifteen years since I last saw the inside of that place. Seemed like nothing had changed either. I couldn't believe it; busted for a tiny chip of crack, just one fuckin' rock. What the hell was going on?

I'd been hustling since I was a kid, making a raise here, a raise there, trying to compete on my own terms. Being careful to stay in my own corner and look after number one. Now I was well into my thirties, on the last lap where it really counts, and I had to worry about not going to jail. Where was the progression?

The cops had been running me down for months, trying to stick me with a supplying charge. They kicked down my front door so many times they must owe me a small fortune in repairs. Then they busted my punters and even brought in the Regional DS to set up some phoney 'operation' where they spent the whole day following me. They were like vultures watching and waiting.

The plan was to arrest as many punters as possible and hope that at least one or two of them would, in order to save themselves, make a statement against me. Others went and busted my house again and thought that if they didn't find any collaborating evidence there then at least those statements would be enough to convict me.

But unknown to them the punters were on my side and would've done anything to keep me out of jail and the drugs flowing. So my counter-offensive was already in place. I wasn't quite as expendable as those regional boys thought I was.

In fact, as far as my punters were concerned, I was priceless, 'cause without me they had nothing. The terror of facing their daily grind 'straight' was unimaginable.

One day Greedy leapt out of the car in the middle of Lumb Lane and confronted his pursuers: 'What the fuck d'you want with me?' he screamed at them, loud enough for anyone else on the street to hear. 'Why are you harassing me like this?' The cops were stumped, completely taken by surprise, and didn't know what to do. They hadn't prepared to make an arrest so soon but what else could they do?

Surely they had to know it was a wind up, but I suppose, under the public gaze like that, they felt they had no other choice. They dragged Greedy down to the station and strip-searched him, but of course they didn't find anything.

The other half who'd searched my house didn't produce anything either, no drugs, no statements, nothing. As a consequence their operation was abandoned.

During all of that I got a call from a punter who'd been told by another punter to warn me about what was going on. That information went through two different people, almost strangers to each other, so as to keep their supply on tap.

So, yeah, the police had been on my case for a long time but they never ever found anything on me. I was always one step ahead of them. Until I went and landed myself with Spencer. He handed me over to them on a plate. But still I wasn't sure . . . was it him or wasn't it?

I told myself it couldn't be true. Not Spencer, my main man. I'd grown up with him like he was my own brother. I'd sacrificed so much for that bastard and this was how he repaid me. I could understand 'dog eat dog' and 'the best man wins', and all those cliches, but what kind of deal is it when your own man turns you in? Yet I still tried to compromise the truth and make excuses for the man. I daren't go anywhere near the thoughts buzzing around inside my head, so instead of confronting the issue I tried to think of something else.

The court case, when it finally happened, was an altogether different affair and took me completely by surprise. I was expecting to go straight to jail and had prepared myself for the worst. But on the day I felt in pretty good shape and stood there in the dock no longer fearful of what my sentence might be. I'd already received a fine and points against my licence for the driving offences, at a previous hearing, so the trial that day was all about the possession charge. But since Bradford City Council hadn't got its shit together and the crown court was still out of action I opted for the local magistrates court rather than Leeds Crown. Perhaps it would've been smarter if I had taken my 'Not Guilty' plea to a crown court jury, especially when you consider those so-called magistrates courts used to be known as the police courts. To some degree they're still under police influence today.

As it happened I didn't feel that I stood a chance

against 'Smith' and that fuckin' scam of his but at the end of the day I got the best possible result. It couldn't have been any better.

The prosecutor stood up and presented her case, detailing my cat and mouse games with the police, how they'd spent the last two years scoring crack cocaine from me in an effort to collect evidence for a future arrest and how I'd pre-empted that arrest by falling into their open arms with a rock. Wow! That was a new one on me. In any court room you can always expect some verbal from the police but I still wondered where the hell I was when they were busy scoring their cocaine from me?

In the absence of any real evidence against me the cops did their very best to fabricate some. I began to think that any minute now that curse of the police courts was about to come into its own. The prosecutor sat back down and was already preparing her papers for the next case. I was amazed. Was that all they had on me then? Was that it?

I couldn't understand the reasoning behind the set up, what was it all about? But of course I should've known, they didn't have anything on me because Spencer hadn't given them anything. All he'd done was leave that rock for them to find in the glove compartment. That's what he'd been told to do and that's exactly what he did.

And even though he might've been central to the police's case he hadn't dared to make a statement against me, if at all they'd asked him for one, and he definitely wasn't going to appear in court because that would have revealed not only his own role but would also have implicated him too. The very last thing the police wanted was for me, or anyone else, to know that he'd been forced to sell me out, otherwise they'd never be able to use him again.

The court accepted I had nothing to do with the car, other than the fact that I was the one caught driving it. Legally if the car wasn't mine, then anything found in it wasn't mine either, unless it could be proved otherwise.

So without Spencer's testimony, and only circumstantial evidence against me, I was home free. The magistrates didn't even bother to retire before delivering their verdict of 'Not guilty'. The relief was indescribable. If 'Smith' had had his way I would've been facing a lengthy prison sentence. He knew that rock had nothing to do with me but what did he care? After eighteen months of running around in circles and having the piss taken out of him he thought that he'd finally caught up with me and certainly had no intention of letting me go. But as it was I did get away.

Still, I didn't hang around showing everybody how clever I was, I got the fuck out of that court room as fast as possible and went to look for Spencer. I needed some answers. I just couldn't find him anywhere, though. It was as if the bastard had dug a hole and buried himself. Then one day this woman phoned me for a rock. I went to deliver it to her and found him outside her house playing football with the kids on the street.

His eyes popped when he saw me. Looked like he was about to shit his pants. He fought hard to keep control but lost it, then came back at me fighting. But he didn't have a leg to stand on and he knew it. The truth was written all over his face. That was good enough for me, told me all I wanted to know. Later for you too Spencer, old friend.

Conversation

Ellie's apartment. Late night/early morning

After a hectic night working the beat, Maureen takes a break from work and calls in to see Ellie for a chat and a cup of tea. She has some good news to report.

MAUREEN: Me and Dave went for an interview at that Face-to-Face rehab centre last Thursday. It's down in Brockenhurst, right next to Southampton, in the middle of the New Forest. It's bloody lovely. We walked into this fuckin' big mansion and it was like walking into a smack-head's house with all these paintings and anti-drug posters up on the wall. It's a really good atmosphere, you know. There's about eight people that run the place; the guy in charge is an ex-junkie, everyone else is straight. But the thing is they're all so *understanding*, you know what I mean?

ELLIE: Oh, I know, it's too fuckin' much, isn't it?

MAUREEN: It'll cost them £17,000 just to keep us there for six months – me, David and two kids. They can't afford to fund Mysti, our other daughter, so my mum's agreed to look after her. It's doing my head in but my son loves it. Apparently he's the only little boy there amongst all those girls so he's gonna have a great time. But they are *so* strict. You've got to be in bed by 11 p.m. but if you can't sleep you're allowed back for an hour or so. I think they give you a Mogadon or something.

ELLIE: Mogadon? Shit, they make you lose your memory, don't they?

MAUREEN: Then you've got to be up at 7 a.m., have breakfast, and go out to work for the day. They grow their own food, do all the building work and everything. They were building a pottery room when we were there. But how do you manage to work when you're feeling so rough, for fuck's sake!

ELLIE: We used to get woken up at the Bridge Project. Nial, one of the workers there, used to wake us up with cups of tea. Anyway, one of us had been home and come back with some smack. We must've gouched out that night from not having any gear for ages and in the morning Nial came in with these cups of tea! I could see the fuckin' dope, and a wrap, sitting right there in the middle of the floor. You'd have had to be blind not to see it. And you know that feeling you get, like when your heart is pounding away in your mouth? Well he came upstairs with the cups of tea, steps right over the gear and the dope, puts the tea down, steps back over the gear and the dope and fucks off back downstairs again! I could not believe it!

MAUREEN: Yeah, but they're really strict down there,

you know, you're not even allowed a joint, not even a drink. And they have room searches every day so it's a bit like being in the nick.

ELLIE: We weren't allowed to drink there either, but we got the rules changed.

MAUREEN: But the rules are stupid anyway 'cause if you're not in there for drinking then you should be allowed to have a drink when you want one.

ELLIE: Yeah, but it's the sort of situation where you're gonna find out who're the alkies and who aren't. People do swap addictions, don't forget.

MAUREEN: Well Dave's an alkie, anyway. I mean, he doesn't *have* to have a drink but if he can get one he'll get it any way he can. There's everything you could want there, swimming pool, the lot. But I won't be in no fuckin' swimming pool. It'll take me months just to get used to it. But there's all these people who've been there three and four weeks, and they're laughing and joking like they were never addicts or junkies.

ELLIE: How much does your social money go down to?

MAUREEN: We'll get £13.90 a week plus our Family Allowance and David gets his invalidity benefit, so we'll be on nearly £60 a week, which isn't bad really. But we're not allowed to have it! For the first month they keep it in the safe 'cause they think that if we have it in our pockets we're more than likely to go out and score. We're allowed money for cigarettes and tobacco. But as soon as we go in we're taken straight off the methadone and put on a two-week course of this other drug. I can't remember the name of it, but it does stop the stomach cramps. But I think we've fucked it already 'cause we've done eight days of methadone in just two days! Last night was terrible. Dave's in bed moaning and groaning that he couldn't sleep so when I told him to shut up and do his methadone he finished it *all* off. This morning he's groaning and moaning again 'cause he's got none left. I said, 'Did I stand there and pour it down your neck?' I think we've done really well so far 'cause we haven't had any smack all day. It's not so bad when you're out and about, at least I know damn well I'm gonna get some – and I'm not going home 'til I have got. So I'm not worried about that. We're supposed to be there in four weeks, but my habit's getting worse. I mean, they're reducing us down to 20 mls. That's the level we've got to be at to enter the rehab. But to counteract that reduction we're doing more smack, so it's not really working. I've even got somebody in Keighley I can score from now. It's fuckin' stupid. The only reason it's not working is because we're picking up our methadone twice a week now, instead of daily. We've got no willpower, that's what it all boils down to. So, realistically, I don't think we'll finish the detox.

ELLIE: Why? I mean it's not as if you're just down the road, is it?

MAUREEN: No. Well that's one of the things we've got going for us. I mean, we're so far away from anyone we know who we could score from. I know how to get on a train and go looking for it but I'll have no money, will I?

ELLIE: In Bridge House I used to go over to Manchester to score all the time. It only took three quarters of an hour to get there, jump in a taxi, go over Moss Side, score the smack and then take it back to the project. I'd only be out for the afternoon.

MAUREEN: We could've gone to the Coke Hole Trust, that's another detox unit, but they just take all the responsibility off you, which is ideally what you want when you're withdrawing. You definitely don't wanna look after the kids. But that's one thing I've got to admit, the kids keep me going more than anything else. If it wasn't for them I'd be in fuckin' hospital, you know what I mean? In that Coke Hole Trust the adults sleep in one building and the kids are in a different wing altogether, so really you're not keeping that family unit, are you? Where we're going the kids are our own responsibility. But I'm gonna have to get myself together. I'm gonna start picking up my methadone daily, so at least I won't fuck up on that, and I'm gonna have to try and stop using brown. I've come out today to hustle some money and try to get some smack together but that's only because we've got no methadone left. I'll tell you something, though, crack has knocked my brown habit down by half. I don't care what anyone says, it's all up here, in your head. I mean, look at all them people giving it, 'Ooh, I was really ill last night, the pain . . . the pain . . .' It's all just so much crap, it's unbelievable!

CONVERSATION

ELLIE: In the refuge, when I used to work at the One-in-Four Project, we used to get lasses coming in with their 'crack habits'. But there's no such thing as a crack habit. It's psychological and you don't actually withdraw from it.

MAUREEN: No such fuckin' thing as, 'First smoke and you're addicted!' BULLSHIT! It's all psychological, it's a psychological addiction! Okay, it's an addiction, but you're not physically addicted, you're not in pain, you don't feel like you're gonna die, it's all mental. I thought it was addictive until I got addicted to smack.

ELLIE: Yeah, but smack's both, it's psychological and physical – *you need it and you want it*!

MAUREEN: With coke you don't *need* it, you just want it.

ELLIE: When me and Lance were dealing brown we were smoking quite a lot of crack and then when we stopped I thought, 'Oh my God, this is gonna be really hard,' but it wasn't.

MAUREEN: Years ago it was speed, speed, speed, and everyone used to go mad for it. I think that was worse than crack.

ELLIE: Yeah, you do get ill off that stuff 'cause it's physically addictive as well.

MAUREEN: And then again there's the needle . . . that's another addiction.

ELLIE: Wasn't it Paul who was telling us about his needle addiction? He said he used to fix rain water from puddles just so that he could stick a needle in his arm. How ridiculous! And he was telling us about how he used to wash out the cracks in between the floorboards with works full of bleach. I just couldn't listen to him anymore!

MAUREEN: Well anyway, I'm off out to work now. I've got to get some smack and take some home to Dave 'cause he's really poorly and he's got the kids too. If I get a stone I'll come back and we can split it between us. I might even be able to buy you a wrap as well, okay?

ELLIE: Yeah, that'll be nice. I'll see you later then.

MAUREEN: I'm not staying out there too long anyway. See you soon.

Lanre: The Visit

Last night, if Ellie hadn't come home, I'm sure Giant would've died from his overdose. He'd been smoking crack all day, then he did some hash, loads of Valium, and then in the evening he came round to our house and shot up some heroin. After a while he snuck into the kitchen to do another hit and Ellie ducked in after him. Suddenly I heard a THUD, then the sound of crockery crashing to the floor. Ellie let out this piercing scream so me and Giant's friend, Lance, rushed in to see what was happening. Giant was collapsed on the floor. He'd OD'd with the works still in his arm.

What made matters worse was that Ellie had given him the wrap on credit 'cause neither of them had any money when they arrived, although Giant did give up Lance's Social book as collateral. Minutes later he was lying dead on our kitchen floor. He'd gone a really weird colour, kind of putty-like, with his eyes rolled back in his head so that only the whites were showing. A string of saliva hung off the end of his drooping mouth. I noticed how his fingers were all bent up and crooked, like he'd been trying to claw some obstruction, some fatal mistake, away from his chest.

I couldn't believe it, I didn't *want* to believe it.

Ellie checked his body for signs of life; Lance bent down and slapped him hard in the face, then slapped him again; I felt like kicking his head off his shoulders. I was furious. How dare he do this to us. We were supposed to be his friends, people who looked out for him and cared about his welfare. Yet there he was putting all our love to the test and laying on a bullshit trip like that. Ellie had asked him whether he'd used anything that day and he'd said no.

I should've known better than to just take his word for it.

Sometimes, when he's on another one of his benders, he'll lie and tell you what you want to hear just so that you'll leave him alone. He gets so fucked up, it's like he's got a death-wish and just doesn't care anymore. He'll spend days, weeks, wandering from house to house, friend to friend, smashed out of his head on practically anything he can lay his hands on. Then he'll wash it all down with another can of super strength lager. It's a ritual I just can't understand because all in all he's a good guy really, very genuine. That's why we nicknamed him 'Giant' in the most respected sense of the word.

Ellie tried to breath life back into his body whilst I pummelled his chest. She tried to lift him up off the floor and sat with his head resting in her lap, but he was too heavy. She couldn't hold him and manoeuvre herself at the same time. So Giant slipped back down along the wall and ended up flat on his back.

He'd already stopped breathing and his lips had turned blue.

'This cannot be happening!' I ranted as I walked around his body, giving Giant the evil eye. I was beginning to freak out. How was I gonna explain this one?

Ellie wanted us to help her manoeuvre him into a more comfortable position, but the Monk suggested we dump him out in the street.

She screamed at us to shut up. 'It's not his fault!' she yelled at the Monk, who ought not to have been thinking of dumping on his friend like that. 'It's the medication he's taking.'

'Yeah right,' I snapped back at her. 'Like Valium, dope, crack . . .' I could sense my overreaction but felt powerless to do anything about it. Giant was lying dead on our kitchen floor!

I worried about the cops busting in and finding him there. I worried about how that would look the next day, how his death would be received on the street. I was beginning to worry about everything. The Monk tried to stand him up and walk him across the floor, but again Giant was too heavy and slipped out of his grasp. Tears welled up in Ellie's eyes. I felt a hot then a cold flush snake through my body.

I had to think – *think* – what to do, but I knew it was too late, we'd lost him.

My hands were trembling, shaking almost out of control, as I snuck a signal to the Monk to step out into the living room. We had to get our story straight.

Then, from the other side of the door, Ellie yelled that she'd found a pulse.

'I've got it! I've got it! I can feel a pulse!'

'What!' I ran back into the kitchen, I could hardly believe it.

So then we set about him all over again, searching frantically for other signs of life. The Monk felt a heart beat, although very faint, but definitely a beating of the heart. I couldn't feel anything. I felt his wrist, thought I had a pulse then realised it was my own. Ellie continued pumping his chest and forcing air into his lungs.

I didn't know what to do. Should I turn him on to his side or leave him as he was? Suddenly he made a sort of gurgling sound which progressed to a cough, so we decided to turn him over anyway and hope for the best. I couldn't believe he was coming back to us. The relief was almost magical, like nothing I'd ever felt before. We worked on him some more, until we were absolutely sure he was back with us, then left him alone in the recovery position and moved into the front room to contemplate our good fortune.

That was close, too fuckin' close for me. But Giant didn't even thank us or anything, he just cussed us down for spoiling his buzz. I didn't get it . . . I felt well pleased with myself after saving his life. Although it was Ellie who did all the work, I wasn't into him spoiling it for me. For a while back there I really thought we'd lost him. He'd stopped breathing, there was no heart beat and no pulse, how much more dead can you get than that? A minute longer and he might've been thrown into someone's backyard. As it happened, Ellie persevered, so the Monk didn't get his way. But still, that was the sixth time he'd OD'd in her house. Six fuckin' times! You'd have thought that once was enough. And after that first time she should never have allowed him to shoot up in her house again, ever. I had absolutely no intention of giving him the wrap. I dug my heels in, but I was overruled.

Giant and Ellie are buddies, they've known each other much longer than I've known both of them put together. So when he turned up at the house rattling, with tears streaming down his face and flashing Monk's social security book as a sweetener, that sealed his fate. He obviously didn't want us to know the amount of drugs and alcohol he'd consumed that day, but what about himself? He knew, didn't he?

And if it's true about that 'other' medication he was on, then surely he must've known that he was in serious danger of going over. It was only later, after we'd revived him and he was happily describing the 'beautiful and painless life' on the other side, that the truth came out.

So, perhaps he was right after all. Maybe he had every right to be annoyed at us for bringing him back. It seems to me, now, that all we did was give him another chance to go all the way. Maybe next time he'll be successful and there'll be nobody there to 'spoil' it for him.

The Monk

I remember overdosing once, years ago when this guy brought some gear over from China. You talk about percentages and stuff, even when you go to the doctors trying to get some methadone they talk to you about percentage grams of street heroin you've had so they can work out how much to give you. But their stuff is so weak it's timid. Then someone comes over from China with this stuff they call Pink Elephant.

He gave me a turn on, a tiny spot about the size of a match head, and I said, 'Hey, c'mon man, what's that?' But he just wouldn't risk it. He said it'd blow my head off. So I thought, well, why not? I'm going to buy some anyway, this is just a TO.

I cooked it up, fixed it, and that was the last thing I knew. It was the most extraordinary thing ever. There were four other people in the room waiting for me, the guinea pig, to suss it out. We were all putting our money together to buy from this guy.

I tell you, I keeled straight over from this stuff. I just lost the will to live. All I remember is people banging on my chest, breathing down my throat and I had the most awful pain in my chest when I came round. They were screaming at me, 'WALK! WALK! MARCH!' Making me walk around for half an hour at least. I wanted to surrender but they wouldn't allow me to give up. If I sat down I would've died; if there'd been nobody there I would've died. And still they kept on telling me to 'MOVE! MOVE! MOVE! MARCH! MARCH!' But I just didn't have the will. I didn't have the will to lift one foot in front of the other. It was like I just wanted to fade out.

I don't remember having any real feelings of being close to death or being shut off. It was 'just leave me alone, let me go', without any real power of voice. I had no strength whatsoever. In my mind it was just so beautiful, I can't describe it really. I wanted to be left alone so I could stay there. And on the other side they were screaming at me to walk, punching my chest and pulling me. I didn't even get a buzz from it, I was too far gone for that. I was in a sort of nebula, on the fringe of life and death, and I didn't even care. It was wonderful. There was no pain, just a feeling of, 'why should I march? Why should I walk around?'

I was really angry with them when I came round. 'Why didn't you just leave me alone? I was enjoying myself.' I couldn't believe it when they said that I was on the threshold of death. I mean, Jesus Christ, it was just too good to be true. And when I remembered that I only had a match head of the stuff I thought someone was taking the piss.

I didn't get involved in any deals in the end because I fell asleep. The guy didn't trust me anyway; he got paranoid and left, so I had no idea what happened after that and just stayed away from it all.

I try to stay away from the drug scene now, especially here in Bradford because it's a bit over the top. When I was in London I'd use up to three or four grams a day but since 1977 I've been out of the scene. I've had a few mishaps, depressions and things, and relapsed a couple of times but for no longer than six months or so. Although, I must admit, the last time I used any heroin was today. Don't worry, it's not another relapse or anything. I've just had a few problems, you know. It's not anything I can't handle.

Lanre: Relapse

Decisions, decisions . . .

Like a landslide of yesterdays, smart ideas, and broken promises.

My head is in a spin. I'm frightened and so dizzy with fear I dare not open my eyes to see where I'm going. I feel like a puppet dancing to the tune of a stuck second-hand record, caught in the same old groove and repeating that disembodied phrase so often I've worn the damn thing out.

My resolve is crushed, my willpower obliterated, yet still I'm making promises that this time will be different, this time I'll nail it down. I want it so badly it hurts. But how many more times must I pick myself up from the floor, dust myself down, and continue this fuckin' dance following the exact same steps as last time?

The absolute worst feeling now is not being in control of myself anymore. Having some external force govern my life, living in subservience to that fuckin' big H. To him I'm just a reflex action, an echo without a voice or will of my own. I feel like I exist purely in deference to Him, a shadow of my former self. But it wasn't always this way . . .

In the beginning was the thrill and excitement of stepping into a new adventure; daring to shine a light into that dark corner and bring the unknown 'let's pretend it doesn't exist' element to the attention of us all. I thought I had it all worked out. I thought I was in a position to contribute as much to our knowledge of heroin addiction as any other who had gone before me. But I became side-tracked: I got tangled up in the drugs and lost the plot. Now all I feel is the frustration of unfinished business, as though my venture into the hard drug scene was cut off prematurely, long before the truth was revealed to me. But isn't that the essence of our human existence, to explore the unknown, seek answers to our questions and then look for even more questions to ask? What would be the point of it all if we already knew what was to come?

I never envisioned myself as a drug dealer, much less a drug addict. That wasn't my ambition – well it was, but not in the way that the big H had in store for me. The simple truth is that I screwed up.

Or maybe I didn't . . . Maybe I was smart enough as a journalist, with my credibility and knowledge of street culture, to get the junkies' story and then move on. After all my interest was genuine. I really did want to know what it is that separates them from us. What do junkies have, or not have, that makes them different from the rest of society?

I jumped in at the deep end and in no time found myself with an addiction of my own. And just around the corner I was about to learn all there was to know about cold turkey! Perhaps I was too enthusiastic. The facts do speak for themselves: from having the kudos of being the number-one drug dealer on the street to becoming a drug addict myself took exactly two years.

I cannot deny that sometimes I miss the hustle and bustle of my drug dealing years. I miss the money, the buzz and that wonderfully deceptive feeling of being safe and secure. It was quite an ego-trip being the only drug dealer with everyone running after me, needing me to bolster-up their lives for them. Even the drugs were fun for a while. But in truth heroin injected so much misery and disorder into my life that even my own family lost sight of me. That is what I regret the most.

I wasn't innocent, I know that, and neither was I proud of the scams I pulled to get hold of more heroin. They were simply a means to an end and typical junkie M.O. to satisfy my cravings. Unlike some mournful teenager who falls prey to the hard drug scene and all its charms, I walked into my addiction with my eyes wide open. At first I thought it was pretty cool. I was exactly where I wanted to be, right in the middle of the action, and getting the story I wanted. But I became like any other heroin addict on the street who cannot escape their lot; I learned to accept it. Eventually I got sucked deeper and deeper inside, so far down that I almost burst through the other side. By the time I came to depend on heroin to enable me to live a constructive day and suppress the threat of withdrawal, it had taken over my life. My world was turned upside down and I was no longer enjoying the adventure.

Ironically the whole point of my so-called 'adventure' was to explore the lives of heroin addicts. I wanted to understand their fear of cold turkey and perhaps experience the effects for myself. How else could I write about something I knew nothing about? I wanted to write about my own experiences, the truth of the situation, where I was on solid ground. I wanted to write the very best I could give. And yet as my addiction took hold and I finally understood exactly what 'doing my cold turkey' would entail, I found that I'd already learnt too much about addiction, much more than any 'straight' person should know. My fear of the pain that I imagined I'd suffer was so much that I reacted in typical junkie fashion and ran away from it. I delved even deeper and began mixing crack cocaine with my daily fix, trying to escape my fears by adopting a double addiction.

By now I'd stepped so far over the line that I'd forgotten what my original brief was. I'd become more like a character in my own comic strip than the artist in charge of it. But I'm sure that there must've been more to it than that . . .

My drug counsellor once told me that heroin addiction is all about escaping from yourself. It's about not being able to acept some dark secret within, so you try to hide from it, or hide it from you. It seems to me now that that's exactly what I was trying to do – but the truth is there is no escape.

Even if I had managed to sneak away, tip-toe away from myself when I wasn't looking, I would've ended up on the run and would've had to keep on running. But life on the run, and in denial, is no life at all. It would've been much better if I'd dealt with the task at hand and confronted my situation. Instead I flooded my brains with both heroin and cocaine until it felt almost as good as being free. The problem was that it soon became the norm, I felt like a prisoner all over again, and then it was even more difficult to escape the emptiness that followed.

For me heroin was like a love story, which gave the illusion of happy-go-lucky irresponsibility. It was exhilarating and, at the same time, tragic. I, who was professionally so cautious in advance, suddenly felt completely relaxed and free. The lifestyle I'd become involved in seemed to be a lifestyle without shame, without rules and regulations. It was a lifestyle completely – and destructively – free. As a junkie I lived for the moment, doing whatever I wanted whenever I wanted. I could say and feel anything I liked. It just didn't seem to matter anymore. But the curious thing was I never stopped seeing my *real* self in this new guise. I saw myself being a junkie and had the bitter privilege of even being present; of seeing at close hand how I looked, what I said, and witnessing how I behaved. In the end I was so confused that I wasn't sure whether I was fascinated by my newly acquired behaviour or frightened by it . . . probably both.

My last attempt at cold turkey didn't work out, I failed at it miserably and opted for the chance of making some money instead. Your money or your health, what the fuck kind of decision was that?

But not to worry. I'm onto a new one now. Not that old can't-shake-this-fucker-off-my-back metha-done script which I'd be labouring over for the next year or so, but a whole new programme which I've negotiated with my drugs counsellor that should see me through to a successful end.

In Nottingham yesterday the woman at the chemist said: 'This is a particularly high dosage, are you sure this is only for one day?' I assured her it was, grabbed my medication and ran. I had only nine minutes in which to catch my train home. But I was laughing all the way. I felt good and confident. My book project had finally reached an end and I'd just taken on a new assignment with Carlton T.V.

My future, which I thought was in the dustbin, suddenly looks rosier than it has done in years. So perhaps I'll make it this time. This could very well be my last chance. Gently . . . gently . . . one step at a time.

I guess now is a good time to make that decision. The only question is, have I lost my nerve to try it all over again; where do I find the courage?

Lanre: Cold Turkey

DAY ONE

The effort of getting up off the floor, dressing, and venturing out of doors sends sharp warning signals screeching into my brain. I want to submit to these alarm bells, wrap myself up in my blankets and go back to sleep, but I can't. I have to confront this thing. And now it's pissing down outside. God knows how I hate the rain. It seeps into my bones like guilt. I can't even take a bath these days without feeling the need to make a full confession. Even a mere splash upon my naked flesh causes me to shrink away in horror.

Uphill from the shops my back alternates between red-hot agony and dull-ache pain. The phlegm in my chest, nose, ears, and throat feels thick and heavy. I want to hawk it up and spit it out but it's too clinging, like crystallised jelly on my lungs, making it all the more difficult to draw breath and walk.

Someone once wrote that kicking heroin is easy, it's just a matter of how strong you are: 'You kick bed covers for a week or so. You run a little temperature. Then you stand up on your feet and walk.' Yeah, well,

I am up on my feet and I'm walking. Only this snail's pace is unbearable. My nose is dripping thick globules of snot which trickle down into the corners of my mouth. Sweat stings my eyes. Then there are the muscle spasms: uncontrollable tics and twitches that assault my upper body, like some old, broken down hobo suffering another bout of the DTs. I am a physical wreck.

So it's slow, slow up the hill, with every step feeling like a new frontier of pain. But still, not to worry, I suppose I am on my feet and walking. I've got Paracetamol in my pocket and a bottle of Orange and Barley water tucked under my arm. I know where I'm going, I've been here before. I cannot, *I will not* lose this battle.

Didn't get a wink of sleep last night. The muscle spasms and cramps grew worse. I could feel them rippling over my body like parasites burrowing through my skin. I was covered in sweat. Freezing cold rivulets of water ran off my body, soaked through the bed sheets and tied me up in knots. I lay stiff as a board trying not to move, trying to ease my discomfort, but then, all of a sudden, *wham*! Another one. I switched on the light and searched frantically all over the bed but found nothing. Those bastards only come out in the dark. I longed to give myself a good scratch and feel the relief as they burst between my finger nails like popcorn, but I daren't.

At 3 a.m. I went out. My head was throbbing, I couldn't take any more. What was worse was that I'd run out of cigarettes. I don't know how long I tramped around. There wasn't a soul in sight; even the whores had taken the night off. In the end I spotted an old dosser and begged a roll up. But I smoked it too fast and benefited nothing from it. If only I could make sense of all this, see a bit of light at the end of the tunnel, at least then I'd have something more reassuring to aim for.

It's my first day into this thing and I'm already asking myself why I'm doing it. Why am I taking on this pressure when I could simply have left it until later? I was pretty comfortable with my addiction, we were good friends and trusted one another with our secrets. When my troubles became too much to bear alone, my addiction beckoned and comforted me. But what started off as something I did soon became the first thing I did before anything else, then became the only thing I did. It became all too easy to kid myself that I needed heroin because I had such-and-such to deal with, or that I needed a dig before I started work in the morning. Every task was formidable unless I eased my way through with heroin. And then I needed more heroin to do less. It was a vicious circle in which it seemed much easier to get high than to get clean. Surviving the Bradford drug scene was almost like surviving Bradford itself. Now it's about who's stronger, me or the wicked seduction of the big 'H' trying to drag me under. I feel like I've been riding a roller coaster, spinning wildly out of control. Now's my chance to jump off somewhere safe.

DAY TWO

My good friend Leo arrived from London last night, armed with his video camera and full of energy. He's eager to record *everything* on film. We went out to eat and discussed my plan of action for the task ahead. I'm well into my task already and plan to continue as I am, taking each day at a time. Leo suggested that since I'm already hurting I should get into the pain, turn it around, and make it work for me. He reckons I should befriend it, embrace it even. After all 'pain is just another emotion and part of our everyday lives'. Yeah, right, my fuckin' best friend in the world! 'And what do you think of the Balti chicken, not too hot?' 'The mango lassi is good too, isn't it?' It's not easy making your agony into dinner time chat.

We finished our meal and walked back to my place. I was trying to get my head around 'enjoying' the absolute agony I felt in my spine and down the back of my legs, which felt like two ends that refuse to meet and join together. The pain is never in the same place twice and is nothing like it was the first time round. One day it takes a debilitating bite out of my back, gnaws through my spine, and tries to pull my guts out through the hole it's left behind. Or else it's a relentless river of pain coursing through my bones, violating every fibre of my body, a tidal wave beating an agonising drum-roll against my nerves. Whichever way it goes is guaranteed to be excruciating. But then suddenly, cruelly, it offers me a perfect ray of sunshine and, just like that, I'm trying to lift myself up in response. I know it'll work itself out in the end. Like the man said, it's only a matter of time. But as I suffer, my anxiety grows worse. I worry about how bad I smell because of my profuse sweating. Occasionally when the video camera isn't watching I wipe the sweat off my brow and smell it. It smells like things have gone from bad to worse, but I imagine that's a good sign and a measure of the toxins being excreted from my body. Back at the flat the room suddenly starts spinning around. Or maybe it's me. I wonder if I'm finally going out of my mind.

Spencer arrives as arranged and the three of us immediately head off for the town centre to shop for provisions. Spencer leads the way, suggesting a rich wholesome soup as being the best thing to sweat out the devil inside of me. I'd prefer to starve and go back to my bed but Leo's got that damn camera in my face already, so I smile sweetly and say nothing. I'm in pain, my whole body is twitching and shivering uncontrollably and my skin feels like it's peeling itself away from my skeleton. I haven't had any heroin for two days and three hours and already I feel like I'm entering into a state of shock. I'm standing high up on a precipice fighting to hold my balance. I'm trying my best to ignore the pain, tricking myself into believing that the more I suffer the better it is for me but, always, in the back of my mind is the fear of things to come being even worse.

Spencer is here to keep me in line, to afford Leo the space to concentrate on filming and make sure that I don't attempt an escape when the pressure mounts. I just wish he wouldn't presume so much or describe in such graphic detail what he's expecting me to suffer. At least the man's heart is in the right place and he is sincere about me getting through this ordeal. He's a good man. I'm glad he's here. The fact that he's offered to do the cooking as well is a bonus, but now he wants to be my bodyguard, too, and shadows my every move. If I blink he blinks and when I put a foot forward he's got both his feet there before me.

At the market, Frances, on the soul food stall, is in her element. 'Is this gonna be on the tele?' she squeals delightedly. She's loading cassavas, sweet potatoes, callaloo, and yams of every description on to the scales. She's buzzing, cheeks beaming, as Leo runs around her with the camera. All I can think of is my toothache, about how I should've gone to the dentist before I embarked on this even greater distress.

Back home Jason comes sniffing around in the afternoon. He doesn't let on what he's after and claims that he didn't realise I'd started my cold turkey already. I want to ask him for a bag, but how can I? Being my eldest son I suppose I should be setting an example for him to follow, even though he has a raging smack habit much worse than my own. If I'd been in my right mind I'd never even have thought of talking drugs with him like that. Even the mere thought of it fills me with disgust. It's another one of those gut-wrenching routines we shared a couple of times. Junkies always seek out their own kind to hang with – even fathers and sons. Maybe I'll never be able to correct the damage that it's done to us but, in some sick fashion, it's brought us closer together. I remember the day he finally admitted to his drug habit. My mouth nearly hit the floor. One week later we came together and shared a bag of heroin . . . This afternoon, though, he was careful not to mention anything about drugs, although I'm sure that's what he came for. But that wouldn't have looked good in front of Leo, at least not today. Not when I'm attempting to regain my self respect and Jason can see in Leo what his father used to be.

DAY THREE

Zaff, a heroin dealing, junkie friend, came to visit this morning. He stepped through the door and I pulled him to one side, to talk privately, but Leo was suspicious and followed us everywhere. Eventually I got him into the spare room and taxed a £10 bag of heroin off him. Two minutes later he's gone and I'm in my bedroom with the door locked, hastily building a spliff. The spliff tastes disgusting but the relief is heavenly. Within minutes I can feel life returning to my body. I relax back on my bed, kick off my shoes and, as if by magic, the aches and pains just seem to melt away. My head clears and for the first time in days I feel like a human being. But then, fuckin' hell, Leo's at the bedroom door demanding to be let in. Suddenly I'm jerked back to the painful reality of my situation. I leap off the bed, frantically waving my arms, trying desperately to clear the smoke, but he's in the room now and demanding to know what's going on. I can't look him in the eye. I feel ashamed. And to add insult to injury a pile of lies fall out of my mouth. But my lies fall on deaf ears. He's not stupid. Even if he's not familiar with the smell of heroin insulting his intelligence he knows exactly what my little tête-à-tête with Zaff was about. He can hardly believe I'd pull such a stunt and is reluctant to admit it even to himself. I can't believe it either. One minute ago I was on top of the world and now, suddenly, I'm right back at square one. Leo walks straight over to the ashtray, picks out the burning end, which is still spewing smoke into the room, and stands there confronting me with the evidence. I can see the hurt in his eyes, the abject disappointment. And still I'm trying to convince him that it's not what he thinks it is.

Minutes later Spencer, who'd been out on an errand, returns and is filled in on what I've been up to. Then they call my drugs counsellor while I'm still hiding in the bedroom thinking that this sorry episode is getting out of hand. Naturally I'm expecting Spencer to come in and give me a hard time too but he steps into my bedroom laughing. I can see there is a seriousness in his eyes and that he isn't necessarily taking the situation as light-heartedly as it appears but his laughter throws me off balance. Leo follows him in and after a minor interrogation from them both, in stereo, they decide to give my room a thorough search, just in case I'm hiding something else they ought to know about. I'm getting a little pissed off at this heavyhandedness and begin to feel like a prisoner again. I do understand why they're dealing with the situation as seriously as they are. After all, the whole purpose of this exercise is to be sure that I clean up my act and leave drug addiction forever. But I'm still hurting, so what can I do?

Later in the night I spy Spencer fast asleep in the front room, sandwiched between two armchairs and with my door keys in his back pocket. I don't need to go out. Leo has finally surrendered to his own sleep. He retired to his bed immediately after I did but I still waited at least an hour before making a move. Mentally, I apologise in advance to them both for what I'm about to do. They've been adamant that I succeed in this cold turkey and have done their utmost to help me through it but I'm going to drop a big shit right on top of them! What else can I do? The need has already started.

I sat with Leo a couple of mornings ago as he broke up all the old syringes to ensure that I don't re-use them. But I know where there're some that he didn't find. In a kitchen drawer, behind some junk, I find what I'm looking for. It only takes me a few seconds to retrieve a couple of old, and probably unsafe, filters that I meant to throw away but didn't. I grab a spoon and water then sneak back into my bedroom and push a chair up against the door. Within minutes I'm sliding the needle into my vein and pressing down on the plunger. I sit back and feel relief spreading through my body as the Devil begins his work.

This is a real chickenshit way of dealing with my problem, I know, but there is a guilt shared by junkies, a sort of collective shame about what we are, what we've become, what we're prepared to do to escape the dread of cold turkey, which condemns us to the very extremities of society and makes our shame invisible to all but ourselves. Only another junkie knows that need and that dark secret. It is a complex business. I cannot even begin to explain. Sometimes I'm fearful of going to sleep at night 'cause I know that I'm gonna be waking up in the morning needing a fuckin' kick-start just to get out of bed and face the day; then spending the rest of that day withdrawing again; waking up in the night, long before the first light of day, soaked through and silently screaming my way through yet another psycho-nightmare.

DAY FOUR

Woke up this morning in the foulest mood, drenched in sweat, aching through and through, and with eyes that would've stopped even the most rabid of smack-head dope-fiends dead in their tracks. I felt weak and ugly, as though a great depression was weighing me down. And as my mood progressed through a spectrum of dark tones, melancholia forced me to look at the reality of my life. Everything appeared to be colourless, unforgiving, and my health was permanently fucked up.

Had that fuckin' dream again last night, a sort of recurring nightmare of weird gargoyles chasing after me in this mad computer game of life or death. Naturally I chose 'life' and gained access to the next level. But then I found my energy pack was low and my score, the aggregate of my past performances, and my chances of survival, hadn't changed. So now I'm down to my last life, my very last chance to complete the game, and I can't move. I start flapping my arms like crazy. Usually in my dreams I'm able to fly away out of danger, but this time nothing happens. In fact, I feel like a dickhead flapping in the face of adversity like this, but what else can I do? I wake up sweating.

The Navaho Indians believe that when a man feels or does something evil it is because a dark wind has entered his soul. Like heroin, it has this way of creeping up on you and taking over your being; of slowly, quietly, getting inside your head, your emotions and even becoming part of your anatomy. It's like a cancer that attaches itself to your insides and mutates your blood cells, so that you and it become one. Heroin robs you of everything: your family, your loved ones, even yourself. What's worse is that it gives nothing back in return – not even the guarantee of making you feel better. I never did get a buzz, or a gouch. In fact, I hardly felt anything at all. But when my explorations took a bad turn and it got a grip on me, everything else went wrong too and I came to depend on it.

I never set out to become a drug addict. I don't think anyone does. I simply woke up one morning sick and realised that I was addicted. That's how I got messed up, feeding myself more heroin, more methadone, more opiates . . . My tolerance became so high I needed even more just to make me feel better, to make my body function in a normal way. And, like I said, even then there were no guarantees. When I look back over the period when I was using quite heavily, nothing comes to mind. Not one single day or a single hit stands out from the others because they were all exactly the same, and that sameness very quickly becomes a blur. Now I understand this cold turkey is exactly the opposite to the rush I'd get from a snowball, and just as it was impossible to detach myself from that rush so it is impossible to detach myself from these withdrawals. The two are intricately linked opposites, like Yin and Yang.

So why is it so difficult to stop using smack altogether? To be honest I really don't know. Perhaps my life, such as it is, has been too fuckin' painful without it. And to clean myself up, as I'm trying to do, seems to take forever. I mean, I'm on my fourth day already and I'm told that I'm still only at the beginning. But there are still times, even today, when my concentration slips and suddenly I catch myself thinking heroin and cocaine. Sometimes if I try real hard I can even taste the drug working the back of my throat. The intensity is so strong I end up dreaming about the stuff at night, then wake up in the morning exhausted. Even when I've been without it for a couple of days I still find myself creeping around at night, searching the house for used filters, old spoons, any trace of the drug that I can use. If I'd really put my mind to it, this week could've been a success but the drug is in my head now and, try as I might, I cannot ignore it. If I do try to ignore it my body will punish me.

Meanwhile my own aches and pains are worse than they've ever been. I've spent most of the morning sitting on the toilet with diarrhoea and the afternoon with my head down it, vomiting. It feels like I'm being fucked from both ends. I feel fucked up and desperate. I can't take any more of this.

I've decided that enough is enough, I'm getting out of here. I want them to know that they haven't let me down, that they did their best . . . But Spencer just laughs at me again. That bastard is so fuckin' sure of himself. He made a wicked curry for him and Leo today whilst I'm still stuck on that fuckin' soup. If there is one thing this jailer can do it's cook. Leo looks more concerned. I think he's beginning to understand how serious I am. Spencer is still smirking as if to say, 'Shut up, Lanre. Sit down.' Well fuck him, I'm going. I make a move towards the front door and as quick as a shot Spencer is in the hallway blocking my path. I struggle to get past him and we almost end up tussling on the floor. Leo is standing over us with that camera again and I'm really getting pissed off now. That bloody camera, it's been on me right from the start, I feel like smashing it to pieces. Somehow I make it to the front door and find that my luck is in: the keys are there.

But then Spencer does a move on me (where the fuckin' hell did he learn that?) and I end up on the floor again. He picks me up and throws me on his back, then carries me into the front room like a baby. I feel too weak to fight him anymore; I'm aching everywhere. Back in the room Spencer flings me down on the sofa then gets back to his meal as though nothing had happened. Leo looks visibly shaken. My heart goes out to the man. I love him dearly, but I've got to get the hell out of here. After their meal Spencer asks if I'm okay and goes on to explain the rules, but I pretend that I'm not interested. Then he offers to make me a warm drink before I take my Clonodine and sleeping pills, then jump into bed like a good heroin addict who's determined to make it through his cold turkey should do. Spencer is in the kitchen, Leo is changing film, and with the devil on my side I make a desperate lunge for the window. I manage to drag the thing open, and with one foot inside and the other on top of the bay window below, I can smell the night air. Then I'm gone.

Epilogue

ELLIE: finally escaped the Manningham drug scene and now lives in Leeds with her daughter. Although she continues to use heroin 'only occasionally', she visits Bradford once or twice a week to score and is still nursing a full-time drug habit.

LANCE: broke off his relationship with Ellie in the summer of 1994 and moved back to Suffolk where he lived until he was hospitalized with cirrhosis of the liver. Just months after being discharged he died, alone in a caravan, from a methadone overdose. RIP.

GIANT: died from a heroin overdose 23 August 1996. He was forty-five years old. RIP.

SPENCER: dropped out of sight and was not heard from again until I called him to help with my cold turkey. He now lives in Bradford with four of his ten children and is said to be 'actively seeking work'.

GREEDY: arrested and charged with intent to supply class 'A' drugs in the 'Operation Gem' bust of 1996. After completing a three-and-a-half year prison sentence he returned to Bradford's Front Line where he continues doing what he does best.

MIKEY: sentenced to prison soon after the 'Operation Gem' bust, but not connected. Returned to Bradford and is said to be on a 'nice little earner'.

MOPIC: has not been heard from since our strange encounter with Sonny, although I do occasionally get word of him. He does still, by all accounts, continue to support a voracious crack habit.

SADIE: after a brief spell in HM Prison, Sadie is still working the beat to support her drug habit and pay off her debts. She has a new boyfriend, currently serving a four year prison sentence, and hopes the authorities will one day give them permission to marry.

MAUREEN, DAVE, AND THE KIDS: were last heard from shortly before they, as a family, entered a rehabilitation centre somewhere in the Midlands. According to reports they are all doing well.

THE MONK: after addressing the issue of his mother's death and his own drug problem, Monk has since cleaned up his act and moved out of town. He now works as an accountant.